A TIBETAN ON TIBET

Mr. and Mrs. Paul Sherap and Son.

A TIBETAN ON TIBET

BEING THE TRAVELS AND OBSERVATIONS OF MR. PAUL SHERAP (DORJE Z0DBA) OF TACHIENLU; WITH AN INTRODUCTORY CHAPTER ON BUDDHISM AND A CONCLUDING CHAPTER ON THE DEVIL DANCE

By

G. A. COMBE

GYAN

Published by

GYAN

Gyan Publishing House
5, Ansari Road
Daryaganj, New Delhi-110002
Phone: 011-47034999, 9811692060
E-mail: books@gyanbooks.com

Distribution Network
gyanbooks.com
India, USA, Canada, UK, Australia, France

ISBN : 978-81-212-6669-7 (PB)
First Published, 1926

2nd Impression 2022

Printed at: Gyan Press, Delhi.

A TIBETAN ON TIBET
Author: G. A. COMBE

A
Tibetan on Tibet

Being the Travels and Observations of Mr. Paul Sherap (Dorje Zödba) of Tachienlu; with an Introductory Chapter on Buddhism and a Concluding Chapter on the Devil Dance

BY

G. A. COMBE

C.B.E., M.A. (Aberd.)

One of His Majesty's Consuls in China

DEDICATED

TO

MY WIFE

FOREWORD

By Sir Charles Bell, K.C.I.E., C.M.G.
(Indian Civil Service, retired; Late British Political Representative in Tibet, Bhutan and Sikkim; Author of "Tibet: Past and Present," etc.)

It is with great pleasure that I accede to Mr. Combe's request to write a short introduction to his book. There are many books on Tibet written by Europeans from the European point of view, but only a few which reflect the Tibetan standpoint.

As befits their nomadic ancestry, Tibetans are adventurous and fond of travel. In the present work we are introduced to a Tibetan, who runs away from home when still a young boy, and travels day after day, month after month, across this difficult mountain land, attaching himself first to one party and then to another. Like many of his race he has a quick, receptive mind, and his accounts of what he sees and feels and does, show us Tibet from the inside. It reproduces, in fact, the Tibetan atmosphere with simple fidelity and charm.

I would fain hope that "A Tibetan on Tibet" will give to others as much pleasure as it has given to me.

CHARLES BELL.

PREFACE

TACHIENLU, or Dartsendo, to call it by the Tibetan name of which the Chinese form is a corruption, is a small township nestling at the junction of two mountain torrents in the Sino-Tibetan Border country 8,500 feet above sea-level. Surrounded by snow-capped peaks, it is the last predominantly Chinese town on the road westward from Szechuan, and is regarded as the main Gateway to Tibet from the east. Here the traveller from the Chêngtu plain enters a new and strange country; for the domestic animals grazing by the stream are yak, the party of bold, dirty, gipsy-looking fellows squatting near them are Tibetans, and the white covering on the mountain overhead is there all the year round. Some few centuries ago this region was politically, as well as ethnographically, part of Tibet; and in spite of the fact that peaceful penetration, following military conquest, has given Chinese the ascendency in the town, its flat, prayer-flagged roofs and the crowds of Tibetans always wandering through its narrow streets markedly differentiate it from the ordinary town in China.

Unlike the Chinese, who in general suffer from anhedonia, the Tibetans are a gay, light-hearted people, full of the joy of living, in spite of their rooted belief in the ubiquity and activity of evil spirits. Tall, heavily built, with the free carriage of mountaineers, fond of ornaments and bright colours, the men are swarthy, the women fresh-coloured, and both, judging by the standards of a "higher" civilization, extremely dirty. Their outer dress is a sheepskin or pulo robe, pulled up so high above the girdle that, while it leaves an ample pocket in the left breast, it falls only to the knee, like a Scottish kilt. With both men and women, the shortness of the robe and the use of knee-boots impart a swing and heaviness to their stride very different from the gait of their more lightly-built neighbours.

Shortly after my arrival at Tachienlu in May last year, I was approached by a local merchant anxious to know how far the road I had come by was open, for it was then the bone of contention between two rival Chinese military factions. My visitor was Mr. Paul Sherap, an English-speaking Tibetan, and in the ensuing conversation he unfolded such an interesting story of his earlier years in Tibet that I engaged him as "pundit," as he would call it, to come to me every evening for an hour or two, and discourse about Tibet and the Tibetans. From my point of view the experiment was a great success, as it provided entertainment during the solitary evenings until, in the middle of August, I was obliged to return to Chêngtu. And Sherap also, seated in an armchair and equipped with a cigar and a cup of cocoa, which was "grateful" enough in that crisp air, appeared thoroughly to enjoy recalling the adventurous days of his early youth, and describing with meticulous exactitude the customs of his countrymen. When I suggested that his story would interest a wider public than myself, he welcomed the idea with all the enthusiasm that his outwardly stolid disposition permits.

Gifted with excellent powers of observation and a retentive memory, Sherap showed himself keenly aware of the desirability of accuracy of statement, and more than once in the course of his artless tale paused to point out that his information on such and such a point depended on hearsay. He will pardon me if I mention that his rather quaint speech, pleasantly flavoured with a mingling of pidgin and biblical English, was sometimes open to misinterpretation. To avoid all possibility of misrepresentation I had at one time the idea of reproducing his exact phraseology, but eventually decided that the disadvantages of such a course outweighed the advantages. Echoes of the original unorthodoxy of phrase, however, I have retained in the personal narrative—to help in conveying the atmosphere—and in such descriptive passages as the one dealing with the tribulations of the soul after death, where it seems somewhat appropriate. I should not omit to mention that the major part of Sherap's information was elicited by means of question and answer, a laborious and dangerous method—dangerous, because a hint or suggestion on the part of the questioner is liable to be picked up and adopted without full realisation of all that it involves. In the circumstances this was unavoidable, and I can only trust that any error due to this cause, or to my revision of his English, did not escape his attention when he corrected the draft of the following pages. Before leaving the subject of validity, the only other comments I would make are that, in speaking of the various sects, a certain bias to the Nyimaba is discernible, due no doubt to the fact that Sherap's hermit brother and his lama friend, Pedma Rinchen, were adherents: and again, that too much weight need not be attached to his measurement of distance by time; time is of no consequence to Tibetans, and, moreover, what is a two-days' journey in one set of conditions may easily be five in another.

Sherap's personal adventures were related with singular detachment. He appeared as if gazing, a remote and disinterested spectator, at the events he was describing. Of the physical hardships he must have endured he says nothing, or hardly anything. Although in the course of his pilgrimages he and his lama necessarily travelled for long distances 16,000–20,000 feet above sea level, it is noteworthy that, except for a casual remark about dried turnip which they carried as being "a good thing to eat when crossing high passes," he might just as well have been travelling in a plain. The sole reference to severe cold at high altitudes comes out incidentally when telling of the Mi-gö that visited them in the night in their cave on a mountain top in Bhutan. And the only allusions to the biting winds, of which all travellers to Tibet have so much to say, are in explanation of the short stages made in the Poison Lake region, where "strong winds get up in the afternoon," and again in sympathy with the small boys who had the tsamba blown from their bowls. But it is all part of his philosophy that "the big man" never allows himself to be affected by adversities beyond his control.

As in regard to the physical world, so in respect of the moral, Sherap preserves his objective outlook without commentary or moralisation. His story of how the Chinese swindled him, leaving him penniless and sick among strangers with whose language he was insufficiently acquainted, is the description of some natural phenomenon, like the "strong wind." In the whole text the only moral judgment is that passed on the women of such and such a country, who "are very lustful." And for me the sudden lighting up of a hitherto lustreless eye when he risked this criticism made the expression of disapproval entirely unconvincing—a sop to the conventions. Doubtless his unusual education, lamas and missionaries alternately teaching first Tibetan and then European ways of looking at life, had something to do with this reluctance to pass moral judgments. Professing Christianity, he never spoke without grave respect of lamaism, especially as practised by the Nyimaba. But his education was such as was bound to make him sceptical of much that he saw and heard, and it is not surprising to find him suggesting that the sacred floating island at Lahore is probably built on a raft, or considering that a tranka (about 3d.) was a somewhat high price to ask for one of Nagarjuna's pills, which are guaranteed specifics against going to hell. On occasion the expression of such scepticism is restrained, as in the case of the young woman in the red gown, or in that of the yogi who left the imprint of his foot on the stone courtyard at Pedmayangtse, neither of whom he is willing to regard as ordinary mortals.

In sharp contrast are the steadfast piety and credulity of Pedma Rinchen, to whom his Buddhist faith is a very real thing. It is he who gets the lump on his forehead by enthusiastic kotowing at Budhgaya, who alone braves the danger of circumambulating Milarasba's temple, who dares to talk at midnight with the ghosts at Chumijadsa, and who thinks he descries the print of the Guru's hand on the waters of Lake Nam. His pilgrimage almost completed, he turns back to crown his good works by a six-months' journey to the holy Mount Dise, at sight of which he falls on his knees in prayer, very happy ; and at last arrived home, he cannot long feel "purged of sin," but must off again to far-distant Koko Nor.

A simple, human, kindly old man ! Dangers and difficulties by land are meat and drink to him, but he would not trust himself on the water to see the divine Dorje Pamo, the Diamond Sow. And his distaste for the Bön priests is hardly concealed. He will not let Sherap endanger the merit acquired on pilgrimage by visiting the German mission, yet, when after some years they meet again, Sherap in the meantime having been baptised a Christian, he utters no reproach, nor even embarrasses his former disciple by mention of the subject. "Living in darkness," maybe, but happy in the thought of one day freeing himself from The Wheel and attaining that Paradise of Dewajen, "where there are no rocks and mountains, but flowers in plenty and the sweet sound of birds singing, and all the time he can see Obame's face, very bright and beautiful."

My grateful acknowledgments are due to the Rev. R. Cunningham, of the China Inland Mission at Tachienlu, who not only willingly undertook the dreary task of romanising all the Tibetan words, but also read over the whole manuscript with Sherap ; to the Rev. J. Huston Edgar, F.R.G.S., of the same Mission, who has spent twenty-three years in the regions west of Tachienlu, and is a mine of information on Eastern Tibet—the "J.H.E." of the foot-notes; and to my wife, for many useful suggestions in the final revision of the text.

To Sir Charles Bell, who has spent eleven months in Lhasa on the invitation of the Dalai Lama, and whose authority on things Tibetan is unsurpassed. I am much indebted for a critical perusal of the manuscript and the contribution of a Foreword to Sherap's story.

LONDON, *5th August*, 1925.

CONTENTS

REFERENCES TO AUTHORITIES.

Bell :	*Tibet : Past and Present*—Sir C. Bell, 1924.
Edkins :	*Chinese Buddhism*—Rev. J. Edkins, 1880.
Eliot :	*Hinduism and Buddhism*—Sir C. Eliot, 1921.
Giles :	*Chinese-English Dictionary* / *Chinese Biographical Dictionary.* } Prof. H. A. Giles
Goré :	*Notes sur les Marches Tibétaines*—Père F. Goré in the *Bulletin de l'Ecole Française d'Extrême Orient,* Vol. XXIII, 1923.
Hedin :	*Trans-Himalaya*—Sven Hedin, 1913 ed.
Huc :	*Souvenirs d'un Voyage,* 1924 ed. / *Chinese Empire,* 2nd ed. / *Christianity in China* } Père E. Huc.
Jaeschke :	*Tibetan-English Dictionary.*
J.H.E. :	Rev. J. Huston Edgar, F.R.G.S., Tachienlu.
N.C.B.R.A.S. :	*Journal of the North China Branch of the Royal Asiatic Society.*
R.D. :	*Buddhism*—Rhys Davids, 1894.
Rock :	*Land of the Lamas,* 1891. *Notes on Ethnology of Tibet,* 1895—W. W. Rockhill.
Sandberg	*Tibet and the Tibetans*—G. Sandberg.
Teich :	*Travels in Eastern Tibet*—E. Teichman, 1922.
Wadd. :	*Buddhism of Tibet, or Lamaism,* 1895—L. A. Waddell.
Williams :	*The Middle Kingdom*—Wells Williams.

ORTHOGRAPHICAL NOTE

BY

The Rev. R. CUNNINGHAM, *China Inland Mission, Tachienlu.*

The romanisation adheres as closely as possible to the actual sound of the Tibetan word. In some cases a familiar spelling has been retained at the cost of consistency—as in Dorje, Panchen, Tsamba—and in others a compromise effected—as in Pedma, between the usual spelling Padma and the pronunciation Bema.

Consonants are as in English, but G always sounded hard, as in " go." Silent consonants have been dropped entirely, as their addition would give the word a mere hieroglyphic appearance and only add to the difficulty of reading. Vowels as follows :—

a as in " f*a*r " : agba.
e as *a* in " f*a*te " : Obame, Pedma (French é).
i as *e* in " m*e* " : biwang, Milarasba.
o as in " n*o*te " : Yamdrog, moba.
ö *o-modified* : Chöjong, Chöden (as eu in French " p*eu* ").
u as in " b*u*ll " : burug, druk.
ü *u-modified* : düdro, püto (as u in French " s*u*r ").

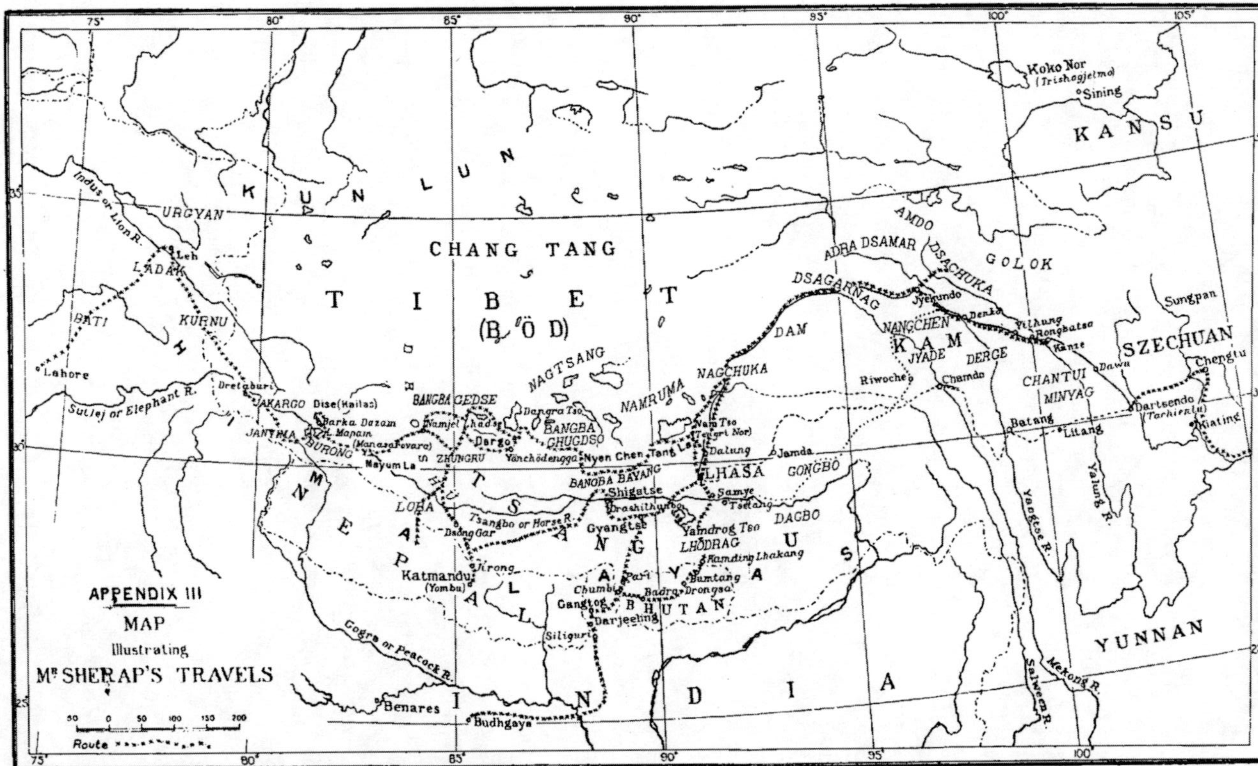

APPENDIX III

MAP

Illustrating

Mr SHERAP'S TRAVELS

CHAPTER I

ASPECTS OF BUDDHISM.

Introductory — I. Primitive Buddhism — The Gospel of Gautama—Karma and Transmigration—The Wheel of Life.—II. Developments in India—Mahayana—Mantrayana—Tantrism. III. Tibetan Buddhism—The Black Bön—Pedma Sambhava—Vajrayana—The Reformation—Tsongkaba—The Four Sects—The Fifth Dalai Lama—Reincarnations—The Present Pontiff.

To the person who thinks of Tibet as "the land of the lamas," it may come as a surprise to learn that, far from being an ancient repository of early Buddhist doctrine, it did not receive the faith until well over a thousand years after Gautama's death. Even then it acquired it fortuitously, so to speak. Had Cleopatra's nose been a little shorter, the whole face of the world might have been changed; and if Tibet to-day is full of men in maroon robes, it is due primarily to the two foreign princesses whom a celebrated king of that country took to wife and who, whatever their domestic relations,* being both agreed on at least one point, namely, the superiority of the Buddhist faith, insisted on his bringing the kingdom up to date and into line with the religious system of their home lands, China and Nepal.

The length of time that elapsed between Gautama's death, about 543 B.C., and King Songdsengombo's mission to India in search of the scriptures, A.D. 642, incidentally illustrates, better than

* The Nepalese princess is represented to have been of a fiery temper, and the cause of frequent brawls on account of the precedence given to the Chinese princess.—*Wadd.*, p. 23, n.

many pages of exposition could do, the extreme isolation on the roof of the world of this solitary people, past whose frontiers, leaving them high and dry, the tide of invasion and counter-invasion ebbed and flowed—Alexander's Greeks, Hun hordes, the conquering Chinese of the Han dynasty—while pious travellers like Fa Hsien and Buddha Bhadra pursued the quest of The Light of Asia. But apart from this, it suggests that after such a length of time the religion brought into Tibet was unlikely to be pure Buddhism; and in point of fact, during those 1,200 years, the gospel of Gautama had changed almost out of recognition.

It is of course only with extreme diffidence that a layman may venture to write about Buddhism. That profound and complex subject can be handled properly only by those who have made it a life study, and who are acquainted with the languages, Pali, Sanskrit, Tibetan, of its sacred books, and by such scholars only if gifted with a keen metaphysical mind. But all that I propose here is to sketch in broad outline such aspects of the origin and development of Buddhism, elucidated by the standard authorities, as may be helpful in explaining what is behind the simple Tibetan mind depicted in the text that follows, which cannot be fully appreciated by the general reader without some such preliminary survey. If in doing so I escape serious fault, I shall be more than satisfied.

I. PRIMITIVE BUDDHISM.

Son of the rajah of a small estate in Northern India, Siddharta Gautama married at 19, and for ten years thereafter lived amidst agreeable surroundings that the normal man might be excused for envying, but which induced in the mind of Gautama, reflecting on the suffering he saw around him, only a great unrest. The birth of a son appears to have acted as the last straw in deciding him to break away from all his pleasant ties before they should become too strong; and at the age of 29, obeying his call, Gautama made what Buddhists refer to as The Great Renunciation—left his beloved wife and child, exchanged his princely clothes for beggar's rags, and took the road as an ascetic, hoping that somewhere in the great world he might discover the causes of human misery and their cure. To the modern pessimist the simple plan of jumping out of the window or into the river would afford an obvious means of terminating life's ills, but it would be no solution to any pessimist brought up like Gautama in the atmosphere of Hinduism, holding the customary belief in transmigration of the soul. In an ascetic life Brahmanism, then the dominant religion in India, professed to find the secret of salvation; and for six years Siddharta lived as few ascetics even in India lived; but austerities and self-mortification were unable to procure for him any permanent satisfaction, and eventually he abandoned them for ever.

Having breakfasted one day under a fig tree, to be known thenceforward by all Buddhists as the Bo Tree, the Tree of Wisdom, Gautama remained seated in meditation all day long, until towards evening the inspiration came to him that whatever misery existed in a world controlled by Karma was due to desire, and that the solution of the mystery of suffering lay in ceasing to desire. When his mind had fully grasped this simple principle, it became peaceful and confident, the whole world changed, everything took on a new and brighter appearance; Gautama had achieved that state of perfect enlightenment called Buddhahood; he had attained Nirvana. The condition would appear to be not unlike that analysed by Professor William James and described by him, for want of a better word, as "saintliness,"* at least in so far as that condition is said to be characterised by an immense elation and feeling of being in a wider life, free from the ties of self, although the "Ideal Power" of which the "saint" has a sensible conviction was in Gautama's case a cosmic law.†

In order to see the problem as Gautama saw it, it is necessary to rid one's mind of all delusions about being a separate self-existing entity, and to believe that life goes on indefinitely, although the poor casket that holds it dissolves into its constituent elements after a relatively short period. It is not very clear what it was that Gautama thought survived when, in the ordinary phrase, a man dies; but he held that, after the death of one body, the concentrated result of all its past thoughts, speech, and action—that is, Karma—finds its way into another body and starts again on the revolving wheel of life.‡

* "Saintliness": see *Varieties of Religious Experience*, pp. 271 *et seq.*

† "It is a common blunder to suppose that Gautama attained Nirvana *when he died*. The texts distinctly state that he did so after the mental struggle" (under the Bo Tree)—*R.D.*, p. 14, note 2.

Nirvana is simply "the extinction of that sinful, grasping condition of mind and heart, which would otherwise, according to the great mystery of Karma, be the cause of renewed individual existence."—*Ib.*, p. 111.

It is "a state attainable in this existence and compatible with a life of intellectual and physical exertion such as he (Buddha) himself led."—*Eliot*, I., 223.

‡ R.D. describes Karma as *that which alone remains* when a man dies, literally

Briefly put, his theory was that (1) existence necessarily involves suffering and sorrow, (2) these are caused by desire—whether for sensual pleasure, for prosperity, or for existence itself, (3) one can escape from suffering by ridding oneself of all such desire, (4) to accomplish this end there is only one way—"The Noble Eightfold Path." These are "The Four Noble Truths"—the essence of Buddhism.

Having eliminated desire, you attain to that condition of sinless calm which is called Nirvana; and further, on the dissolution of your body, you achieve that extinction of life called Pari-Nirvana, after which there can be no re-birth. You have finally escaped from the wheel of life.*

Thus primitive Buddhism resolves itself into a system of self-discipline, in which the individual cultivates a distaste for the hopes and cares of ordinary life. It knows nothing of a Soul, or of God; Arhats, the holy persons who, by eliminating desire, have attained Nirvana, are superior to the gods of Hinduism. It is indifferent to the mystery of creation, to enquire into which is profitless. It acknowledges no form of prayer and it contemns self-mortification and ascetism. It recognises a moral cause in the universe, which is manifested in

his "doing," the result of his action, speech, and thought, good and evil; and goes on to say: "We are familiar with the doctrine of the indestructibility of force—but the peculiarity of Buddhism lies in this, that the result of what a man is or does is held, not to be dissipated, as it were, into many separate streams, but to be concentrated together in the formation of one new sentient being—new, that is, in its constituent parts and powers, but the same in its essence, its being, its doing, its *karma*."—P. 104.

In a famous passage Huxley identifies Karma with "the sum of tendencies to act in a certain way, which we call 'character.'"—*Evolution and Ethics*. But it should be kept in mind that in the Indian doctrine such tendencies were not inherited from earthly ancestors.

* It has often been pointed out that "desire" is not a satisfactory equivalent for the Pali term, which is better translated "lust and craving for pleasure." Buddha did not reprobate good desires.—Cf. *Eliot*, p. xxi, n.

Karma, and which ordains that whatsoever a man hath sown that shall he also reap, although it may be in another existence. Its most obvious difference from our western ethical systems lies perhaps in its dwelling on Being rather than on Doing, on selflessness rather than on self-realisation. But it cannot be called a religion of mere negation. As a modern Japanese writer has expressed it: "It is a negation of the bondage of individual limitations, but also an entrance into the larger world of ideals." And its teaching in regard to "self" probably approximates more to New Testament doctrine than does "self-realisation" as pursued in the west. In practice it seems to work out to this, that while the pure Buddhist does not regard the present as the real world, or his own life as discontinuous from all life—is not in fact living "in time"—the westerner on the contrary, impressed with the reality of this world, its progress towards an end, and his individual place in it, adjusts his ideas and activities accordingly, and in the achievement of his desires wins general applause, provided of course that his desires and conduct in pursuit of them are not of an anti-social kind.

In Buddha's theory, with the Hindu background of the world regarded as an endless repetition, unless you renounce desire—meaning the thirst or craving for existence, pleasure, and success—your destiny, working itself out through your Karma, will be re-birth in a world of sorrow and to be re-born again and again until the breaking up of the universe at the end of the Kalpa or time-cycle. And your re-birth may be into conditions much worse than those of your present existence. If we accept

Buddha—and there would seem sufficient reason for doing so—as the originator of the picture of the Wheel of Life, it would appear that he indicated five different regions (Gati) into which you may be re-born: those of the gods, man, animals, tantalised ghosts, and purgatory, to which was afterwards added that of "The Titans." "But the very gods envy the blessed state of those who, here on earth, escaped from the floods of passion, have gained the fruit of the Noble Eightfold Path, and have become cleansed from all defilement, free for ever from all delusion and all sorrow, in that Rest which cannot be shaken—the Nirvana of Arhatship which can never be lost."*

So, in respect of the theories of transmigration and Karma, Buddha, to start with at least, took on the colour of his Brahmanic surroundings. And we may as well note here that he adopted at the same time the Brahmanic pantheon and ideas about the structure of the universe—with these modifications, that he refused to recognise any divine creator among the gods, all of whom he regarded as mortal and like other mortals subject to the law of palingenesis.

Like the formulators of the "Ten Commandments" and the "Twelve Beatitudes," Buddha made use in teaching of numbered "headings," such as "The Four Noble Truths," which were the foundation of his moral law (Dharma), and "The Noble Eightfold Path," which guides the devotee to Nirvana. But, as already mentioned, he seems to have gone farther, and illustrated his view of life by drawing on the ground a diagram of "The Wheel of Life," which is a very notable feature of Buddhism and is still

* *R.D.*—p. 149.

portrayed on the walls of porticos in most lamaseries in Tibet. The picture, as it has come down to us in its various forms, is greatly elaborated beyond the original, as will be understood from the following description of one recently painted by a professional Tibetan artist.

The Wheel is shown, as usual, clenched tightly from behind in the claws of a monstrous animal that is said to symbolise the hideousness of clinging to life. On the hub are three animals forming an endless chain by swallowing each other's tails. They are—a black pig, a red bird (? dove), and a green snake, representing the three vices of ignorance or delusion, desire, and ill-feeling respectively. Their position in the Wheel signifies that round them and attached to them all sentient existence revolves.

On the panels between the six spokes are painted the Gati: The Lha (gods) Country, where gods and goddesses walk in lovely gardens, live in noble palaces, and pluck the fruit of the wish-granting tree: the Lhamayin (titans) Country, where are the roots and trunk of the tree and whose envious, irascible people war in vain against the Lha: Man's Country, with all its woes depicted, birth and death, the struggle for a bare subsistence, accidents, sickness, the heavy hand of the law: the Animals' Country, still more miserable than Man's, where beasts prey on each other, are shot or trapped by men, or overworked and goaded by him in domestic service the Yidag (tantalised ghosts) Country, haunted by the ghosts of the miserly and gluttonous, creatures with swollen stomachs, thin necks and legs, and flames issuing from tiny mouths: and Nyalwa, purgatory, where savage men with animals' heads drag to unspeakable tortures those condemned by the inexorable Judge. In each of the panels is inserted a picture of Janrezig, the Merciful One, to whom is addressed the prayer for release from the Wheel—Om-Mani-Pedme-Hum.

Although they live for thousands of years, the lotus-born gods at last die miserably: they are of course subject to re-birth and, if they have not been virtuous as gods, their next existence may be in a lower region, even in purgatory (whose Judge, too, may share the same fate). The Lhamayin, who are also lotus-born, do not live quite so long as the gods, and always die fighting vainly against them. These two classes have their abodes on the upper and lower slopes of Mount Rirab, the Buddhist Olympus. The other four are really all here in this world, although many Buddhists believe in a real purgatory situated in the bowels of the earth.

Of much subtler significance are the twelve pictorial segments into which the felly of the wheel is divided, and which represent "The Twelve Causes," although the word "cause" must be interpreted in a very liberal sense, one phase being simply an "emergent" of its precursor. The pictures, with their orthodox designations, are as follows:—

1. A blind old woman led by a guide (Karma): designated "Ignorance."
2. A potter modelling clay on his wheel: "Conformations" or "Predispositions."
3. A monkey climbing a tree: "Consciousness."
4. A man in a boat on the sea: "Name and —Form."
5. An empty house with five windows: "The Senses."

6. Sexual Union : "Contact."
7. A man with an arrow penetrating his eye : "Sensation."
8. A man drinking wine : "Thirst or craving for Existence."
9. A man grasping and storing up fruit : "Clinging to Life."
10. A woman in pregnancy : "Becoming."
11. Birth of a Son : "Birth."
12. A man carrying off a corpse for burial : "Death."

"The Chain of Causation," as it is called, is variously interpreted. Eliot follows Buddhaghosa (*fl. circ.* A.D. 450), who says that the first two links belong to past time and explain the present existence : the next eight analyse the present existence : and the last two belong to future time, representing the results in another existence of desire felt in this existence. Waddell regards all twelve links as referring to one individual life, and supports this interpretation by pointing out that it would almost seem as if Buddha personally observed much of the order in this chain in his ethical habit of cutting the links which bound him to existence. Thus he started with cutting off No. 11 (his son), then No. 10 (his wife), then No. 9 (his worldly wealth), then No. 8 (desire), on doing which he attained Buddhahood, the Perfect Knowledge dispelling the Ignorance which lay at the root of Desire.

There we must leave the Chain of Causation. It is recognised to be one of the most obscure formulæ of Buddhism, and second in importance only to "The Four Noble Truths," but more thorough consideration of it is not required for the purpose of my text.

II. DEVELOPMENTS IN INDIA.

As Gautama's teachings were not written down until 300 years after his Pari-Nirvana, the interval afforded plenty of scope for divergence of opinion over his doctrines, and the faithful were divided as to whether existence was real or merely illusory. A new school arose, calling itself The Middle Path, which denied the possibility of knowing that anything either exists or does not exist. The world was still renounced, not for its sorrow and pain as the older Buddhists said, but for its unreality; and the goal Nirvana, or rather Pari-Nirvana, while ceasing to be extinction of life, was now considered a mystical state admitting of no definition. However, instead of confining salvation to a few only—for primitive Buddhism practically limited salvation to celibate mendicants—the new system offered salvation to all, and for this reason was known by the name of Mahayana, the Great Vehicle. As it also substituted good words for the good deeds of the earlier Buddhists, its appeal was very popular and the primitive faith, that of Theravada, the School of the Elders, became known as The Little Vehicle, Hinayana, a somewhat contemptuous reference to the smallness of the accommodation it offered. But the greatest innovation was the displacement of the agnostic idealism of Theravada by theism. Buddha was worshipped as an omniscient being, enduring from all eternity, a sort of universal essence of a pantheistic nature. And as he had entered Nirvana, metaphysical Buddhas and celestial Bodhisats, or potential Buddhas, were invented, who are outside Nirvana and therefore able to help.

The Hinayana held that, before his last birth,

Gautama dwelt in the Tushita heaven, and that the coming Buddha, Maitreya, is now there awaiting the end of the Kalpa before visiting the earth ; but it admitted no other Bodhisattvas. Mahayana taught that it was in the power of all human beings to become Bodhisattvas and that this, rather than Arhatship, should be the aim of the religious life. Even in Gautama's lifetime his teaching was sometimes ridiculed because it would deprive households of their support and depopulate the country. The new doctrine escaped this charge : it further taught that, although the Buddha had attained Pari-Nirvana, yet the state of Bodhisatship, in which one would still keep in touch with the world and help one's fellowmen, was morally superior. As Professor Rhys Davids puts it, the theory of Bodhisatship is the keynote of the later school, just as Arhatship is the keynote of early Buddhism. The Arhats, being dead, cannot be active ; the Bodhisats as living beings can.

Gautama was now regarded as only one of a series of Human Buddhas, all of whom were manifestations or reflexes of celestial counterparts. One of the earliest forms given to the greatest of the five great metaphysical Buddhas (Tib. Jinas) was Amitabha (Tib. Öbamè), the Buddha of Boundless Light who lived in the paradise of Sukhavati (Tib. Dewajen), situated where the sun sets. The metaphysical Buddhas are almost impassive, but by meditation they evolve active celestial Bodhisats, who possess creative functions and produce earthly reflexes or incarnations in the form of human Buddhas. So Amitabha was said to have evolved the Bodhisat Avalokita (Tib. Janrezig), who in turn produced

Gautama. And the next Buddha to be incarnated will be Maitreya (Tib. Jamba), who is now waiting in the Bodhisat's paradise, Tushita, to visit the earth at the end of the Kalpa, which will be 5,000 years from the rediscovery by Gautama of the truth under the Bo Tree.

Another innovation, long overdue, that satisfied the natural craving for something real and positive in the universe, was the promise that "on the other shore," that is, "in that condition which admits of no re-birth or death, no change or suffering, there is absolute and imperishable existence." Hence the goal now sought by the great body of Mahayana Buddhists, is Dewajen, the paradise of Obame. The almost sharp dispute between Pedma Rinchen and his young friend Sherap on the top of Milarasba's temple is typical of the divergence of opinion among Tibetan Buddhists as to what may happen to them after death.

Whoever originated the Mahayana doctrine, which found its earliest patrons among the Scythians and Indo-Persians, and was recognised by the Scythian King Kanishka's Council about A.D. 100, it was Nagarjuna in the 2nd century of our era who elaborated it and secured its establishment as the orthodox doctrine by claiming for it the authority of Buddha himself. Buddha was made out to have expounded it in a treatise which he confided to the keeping of the Nagas until such time as men should be sufficiently enlightened to understand it.

It is unnecessary to confuse the reader with the names of the five celestial Buddhas or Jinas, but those of the four chief Bodhisats will frequently recur in the following pages. They are :—

Maitreya (Jamba), the Coming Buddha.
Manjusri (Jamyang), the God of Wisdom.
Vajrapani (Chana-dorje), the wielder of the Thunderbolt, Jupiter Tonans, and
Avalokita (Janrezig—he who sees with bright eyes), the God of Mercy.

The last three of the above are regarded by Mahayana Buddhists as Defenders of the Faith *par excellence*, and are called The Three Lords (Tib. rigsum gonbo). Two female Bodhisats must also be mentioned, Tara (Tib. Drölma), the Goddess of Mercy,* and Marici or Vajravarahi (Tib. Dorje-Pamo), the Diamond Sow.

Following the great schism between Mahayana and Hinayana the next development, which affected both sects but especially the theistic Mahayana, was the introduction from Hinduism of Yogacarya beliefs. These embodied the idea of a soul (Atman) and its ecstatic union with the Universal Spirit, the union being achieved by means of a self-hypnotising process to be learned by rule. Mental concentration upon one point with a view to annihilate thought resulted in the eight great magical powers, *Siddhi*, namely: the ability to make one's body (1) lighter, (2) heavier, (3) smaller, (4) larger than anything in the world, and to (5) reach any place, (6) assume any shape, (7) control all natural laws, (8) make everything depend on the pleasure of one's own will. This Hindu doctrine was introduced into Buddhism in the fourth century by Asanga, a monk of Peshawar, who is also credited with teaching the use of spells

* Drölma appears in twenty-one different forms, but her best known manifestations are as the White and the Green Drölma. King Songdsengombo's Chinese and Nepalese princesses were subsequently recognised as reincarnations of the White and Green Drölmas respectively; and Mongols regarded the White Tsar as a reincarnation of the White Drölma.—*Wadd.*, pp. 22 and 359.

(Mantra). Charmed sentences (Dharani) were used as incantations for procuring help in difficulties and "magic circles" (Mangdala) formed by which the divinities are coerced into assisting the votary to reach "the other shore." The Om-Mani-Pedme-Hum formula is of this Dharani order, although it is believed to have originated at a date much later than that we are now discussing. From its use of spells, this system gets its name of Mantrayana, the Spell-Vehicle.

It was about the end of the seventh century that Buddhism underwent a still more notable change through the introduction of Tantrism, a mixture of magic and Shiva-worship specially prevalent in the sub-Himalayan districts, both east and west. Characterised by the worship of the Active Producing Principle as manifested in Shiva's consort Kali, it resulted in wives being allotted to each of the Jinas and Bodhisats, with the exception of Manjusri, the God of Wisdom. These female energies were all manifestations of Kali, generally materialising in at least two forms, one of mild aspect, the other malignant. Further, to aid The Three Lords in defending the faith were introduced Yidam, or tutelaries in the form of demon-kings, repulsive monsters of the Shiva type, with wives equally unprepossessing. The only other novelty we may notice here is the addition of a second active reflex to each Jina in the form of a kingly Bodhisat of mild type, adorned with a crown and jewels : it is needless to give the names of these five "adorned Jinas," excepting that of one, Amitayus (Tib. Tsebame), the Buddha of Eternal Life, who is the adorned reflex of Amitabha. Exclusive of innumerable miscellaneous deities the pantheon now consists of Five Jinas, each with one "adorned reflex," one Bodhisat reflex, and one earthly reflex. Thus we have in one series of the Jina:—

Jina . .	Amitabha / Obame	Buddha of Boundless Light.
Adorned Bodhisat Reflex	Amitayus / Tsebame	Buddha of Eternal Life.
Bodhisat Reflex	Avalokita / Janrezig	Buddha of Mercy.
Earthly Reflex	Gautama	The Buddha.

With its character thus altered, Buddhism was in the last stages of decadence in India when the Tibetan Mission arrived to study it.

III. TIBETAN BUDDHISM.

In the middle of the seventh century of our era, Tibet was still a hermit kingdom, inaccessible even to the Chinese, given over to an animist religion, the Black Bön, which was characterised by devil-dancing and human sacrifices. When, after harassing the western borders of China, King Songdsengombo was finally bought off with the gift of the Chinese princess Wên Ch'êng in 641, at her instance, and that of his Nepalese consort, he sent a mission to India under Thonmi Sambota to study Buddhism and bring back Buddhist books. The result of this mission was the introduction into Tibet of a decadent form of Buddhism, along with a modification of the North Indian alphabet, by means of which the Tibetan language was for the first time reduced to writing. For these benefits Songdsengombo is held to be the most famous of Tibetan kings, although Buddhism for the next hundred years made little progress among his people, who remained for the most part bound in the toils of Bön demonolatry.

The real foundation of Tibetan Buddhism came a century later under another celebrated king, Trisongdedsen, who sent to India for a monk to establish an Order in Tibet. His messengers came back in 747 with Pedma Sambhava, one of the Yoga Tantrik school, native of Udyana, a country to the north-west of Kashmir, that was as famous for magic and wizardry as was Thessaly in ancient Europe. He at once declared war on the Bön demons and, with his thunderbolt and his spells, so defeated and outwitted them that they were all either driven out of the country or incorporated in the Buddhist system as Defenders of the Faith, Yidam, Chöjong, and Gönbo. Thus to the pandemonium of the Tantrik Mahayana was added a multitude of demons of the Black Bön, and on this basis—of Shivaic mysticism, magic, and Indo-Tibetan demonolatry—the Buddhist Pedma Sambhava founded the Order of Lamas and built the first monastery at Samye. So Lamas and Lamaseries came to Tibet. Commonly referred to simply as Maha Guru, the Great Teacher, Pedma Sambhava is now deified and worshipped by the unreformed church as the Second Buddha.

About the tenth century two other importations from India affected what we may now call Lamaism. The first was the theory of Adi-Buddha, a Primordial Buddha, or Creator, who was declared to have by meditation evolved the five Jinas. The second was the practice, by devotees aspiring to the spiritual powers of *Siddhi*, of enlisting the aid of Demoniacal Buddhas and Fiendesses. These two importations came from the Kalakakra system, also known as

Vajrayana or "The Thunderbolt Vehicle"; and Vajrayana is the form of Buddhism now most prevalent in Tibet. In the circumstances, it is remarkable that superior lamas still preserve much of the lofty philosophy and ethics taught originally by Gautama.

The next great event in the history of Lamaism was the Reformation, started in 1038 by Atisha, a Buddhist monk from Bengal, belonging to the Vajrayana school. The chief result of Atisha's efforts was to divide Lamaism into sects. Those who did not accept his doctrine and remained unreformed became known as Nyimaba, or "The Old School," who are more freely than any other tinged with the native Bön practices. The reformed sect was known as the Kadamba; and two semi-reformed sects that sprang up about the same time were designated Karjuba and Sachyaba respectively.

The first of the four sects to become powerful in the country was the Sachyaba. About A.D. 1200 Tibet was conquered by Jinghiz Khan, and seventy years later his descendant, Kubla Khan, recognised the Sachya Grand Lama as head of the Lamaist Church, and temporal ruler of Tibet under himself. This temporal supremacy was maintained until the Mongols were driven out of China by the Mings (1368), who deemed it politic to give the Grand Lamas of the three reformed sects equal rank. But about 1400 a lama named Tsongkaba, reorganised the Kadamba sect under the name of Geluba, and it soon eclipsed all the others in power. He made monastic discipline stricter, insisting on celibacy and frequent services of prayer; and he greatly reduced, although he did not annihilate, the tantrik and magical element in Lamaism. Tsongkaba's nephew was the first Grand Lama of the Geluba; and in order to secure stability of succession to the headship of the sect, the theory of reincarnation of the deceased lama was introduced. Since the practice worked well, it was soon adopted by other sects, and it has so extended that now nearly every great monastery has its own reincarnate lama as its chief, and some have several of these among their higher officials.

As Lamaism enters on its modern phase we find it divided into four sects—the Geluba or Yellow Sect, being the Established Church; the Nyimaba or Red Sect, being the Unreformed Church of Pedma Sambhava; and the two semi-reformed sects, Sachyaba and Karjuba. The Bön religion survives, but it is the White and no longer the Black Bön, and it is deeply impregnated with Buddhism.

Modern Lamaism may be said to date from 1640, when Nagwang Lozang, the Fifth Grand Lama of the Yellow Sect, became Priest-King of Tibet. This ambitious prince sought to justify his exercise of the divine right of kings by posing as an earthly reflex of the Bodhisat Janrezig, whom he also identified with the judge of the dead. He promoted his four predecessors to the same rank, and since his day these identities have been recognised as attaching to the Dalai Lama by all the lamaist sects, who themselves adopted the ingenious idea of divine reincarnation. As a natural sequel various other notabilities were canonised: first of all (in order to secure the loyalty of the people to the Dalai Lama) the popular King Songdsengombo was identified with Janrezig; then Tsongkaba, Atisha, and Trisongdedsen were recognised as earthly reflexes of Manjusri; and so on.

Waddell, who is the authority for these particulars regarding reincarnations and reflexes, adds that Nagwang Lozang proclaimed the Drashilhunbo Lama to be a reincarnation of the lama who had been his spiritual father and adviser; and not only so but recognised him as an earthly reflex of Obame, the spiritual father of Janrezig. Hence the Panchen Lama receives a position second only to that of the Dalai, and is regarded as even more holy, if that is possible, as he is less contaminated with temporal government. But it has been cynically suggested that, in recognising the Drashilhunbo Lama as a reflex of Obame, Nagwang Lozang meant it as a reminder that Obame was a passive divinity, who left the care of worldly things to his spiritual son, Janrezig, reflected in the Dalai Lama.

When the Sixth Dalai Lama, who was hopelessly dissolute, died in 1703, the Manchu Emperor stepped in and assumed the suzerainty, taking over control of the foreign policy. He even endeavoured to introduce a nominee of his own as Seventh Dalai, but the Tibetans successfully resisted this attack on their religious freedom; and the Geluba sect, as the Established Church of Tibet, continued to prosper and its Dalai Lama to be recognised by the other sects as the *de facto* ruler of Tibet and Supreme Pontiff of the Lamaist Church.

Tibet is no longer the Hermit Kingdom that it used to be. Very gradually it is being opened up. The reigning Dalai Lama, Tubstan, 13th in the line, was born in 1876 and has had his share of trouble. Having fled to Peking on the approach of the British expedition in 1904, he remained away from Lhasa for five years; and had no sooner returned to his capital when, in 1910, he had to seek asylum at Darjeeling on the approach of a Chinese expedition. As a result of the 1911 revolution in China, Chinese troops were driven out of Tibet, and the Republic, although still claiming suzerainty, does not carry the same weight that the Manchu Emperors did.

CHAPTER II

SHERAP INTRODUCES HIMSELF.

I take the caravan road to Lhasa—Am entered at Drebung Monastery—Run away from Drebung—The Chumbi merchant—At School at Gangtog—At the Ghoom Mission—Pedma Rinchen—I return to Ghoom, am baptised, and go to Calcutta—With Chinese to Shanghai, am deserted, but rescued by missionaries—Marry and settle in Dartsendo—The Derge printing-press—Revisit my birthplace—Pedma Rinchen again.

I WAS born at Rongbatsa, in the Kanze district, in the Fire-Hog year (1887),* my father being Mongolian from Little Karchim, between Kalgan and Dolon Nor, and my mother pure Tibetan. The name given to me at birth was Dorje, meaning "Thunderbolt." While I was still small, my mother wanted me to become lama, "because no work, plenty to eat, and without sin." So when I was six years old the lama was sent for and he gave me the religious name Zödba, meaning "Benevolence." My mother died a year later, and my father when I was nine. I had one brother and one sister. My brother was a good lama of the Nyimaba sect, a hermit; my sister was married and I went to live with her, but she was not caring very much for me. All the time I wanted to go to my mother's brother in Sikhim, who was in business; also it is Tibetan custom that everyone must go at least once to

* The Tibetans reckon dates according to a short cycle of twelve or a long cycle of sixty years. Each year bears the name of one of twelve animals, and in the long cycle the date is indicated by combining the name of the animal with one of the five elements, wood, fire, earth, iron, and water. 1924 is the Water-Mouse year, and is the first of a new 60-year cycle.

Lhasa and see the Potala and the Buddha in the Jokang, and be purified of sin. As my sister refused to allow me to go, after I had stayed with her for a year or so, one night I took some tsamba,* an extra coat, an extra pair of boots, some spare leather to mend them, and forty rupees,† and ran away.

I followed the Lhasa road, sometimes walking, sometimes lying down to sleep, until at daybreak I came upon many tents and many lamas. An old lama enquired where I was going and then said, "I go to Lhasa too, come with me." I travelled with this lama for a fortnight, but it was not very agreeable. Daytime he gave me plenty things to carry and he was not very kindful. One night, when all were in a cave at the river side, I escaped up the mountain and slept in the forest. Next morning at sunrise they looked round for me, being ready to start, but could not see me, although from the edge of the forest I could see them and even hear them tell each other "Dorje run away." Then, without more delay, they all set off, not troubling further about me.

I waited until nearly mid-day and then left that place, and a little farther on fell in with a nomad family who were preparing a caravan for Lhasa. The nomads were very kindful, gave me sour milk and tsamba, and allowed me to go with their caravan. I travelled with them for about half a month, when we met a lama with one or two servants and several horses. He said to me: "Don't go with the caravan, come with me." He gave me food and a horse, and so by and by, after a long journey about which I remember very little, we came to Lhasa.

* Tsamba is parched barley; for mode of cooking, see p. 130.

† Rupees: these were Indian coins; at that time (1897) the Chinese rupee, which is worth about 9½d., did not exist.

This lama had a good friend in the city, a high Tibetan official, at whose house we stayed. He was in charge under the Debazhung* of the supply of butter for the lamps in the monastery at Samye.† During the month that I lived in his house he visited Samye on this business, and took me with him. Across the river from the monastery is the village of Tsetang, with a Geluba monastery, and behind the monastery a mountain called Gönbori, that is "The Gönbo's mountain." In this mountain is a cave known as Srin-mo Pug, "The Demoness's cave," where once lived Dra-srin-mo,‡ the rock demoness, who is said to be the ancestress of all Tibetans, her husband being a monkey. It is empty, and people round about do not speak much of it. The official told me the story and so did my lama friend.

This official asked me whether I wished to go back to Rongbatsa, but I told him I wanted to go to India. He then offered to adopt me, as he had no son of his own, and, if I cared, to send me to Drebung§ to become a lama. My lama also thought this a very good plan. The official gave me plenty very good clothes, some of them of silk, and sent me to Drebung monastery, where an old lama was engaged as my gegen (teacher), and I had to read books all day. The gegen was

* Debazhung: the Lhasa Government.

† Samye, the oldest monastery in Tibet, is 30 miles south-east of Lhasa, near the north bank of the Tsangbo or Brahmaputra, known to Tibetans as the Horse River.

‡ The story of Dra-srin-mo and the Bodhisattva monkey is told with more detail in the next chapter.

§ Drebung monastery is the largest in Tibet. Waddell says: "It is situated about three miles west of Lhasa and contains nominally 7,000 monks. It is divided into four sections clustering round the great cathedral, the resplendent golden roof of which is seen from afar."—(p. 269). It was the residence of the Grand Lamas of the Geluba until Nagwang-Lozang, the Dalai Lama, built Potala in the 17th century.

very rich, but dirty, and not a good lama. All the time he was eating dried meat and good tsamba and butter-tea, but gave us (he had three pupils) only black tea* and poor tsamba. Night time he did not sleep until 11 o'clock, reading prayer books till then, and we had all to wait in the kitchen until he was finished. He woke us before daybreak to make us read prayer books and, when he went out, he locked us in, just like a prison. I thought, "I don't want live here; must run away."

So one spring morning, after I had been in Drebung for about half a year, I left the monastery before daybreak and walked some miles to the plain, where are many poplar trees. I stopped to consider where to go. I had brought with me a small bag full of tsamba and butter, and was in my draba's† dress—that is, red blanket, red skirt, and draba boots, all of which I had received from the gegen—but had left my high yellow cap behind. When the sun had risen, many lamas began to come along the road on their way to Lhasa, and, fearing they should see me, I climbed one of the poplars and sat hidden among the branches. As they passed underneath I heard them mention my name: "This morning Dorje was not in his room; the gegen is searching for him in the monastery." When all had disappeared, I decided that I must get away at once, else the gegen would catch and beat me. But again I thought, he has no reason to beat me: I have not taken away anything. That official gave me a box full of good clothes, but I have left them all

* "Black tea" is simply tea with a little salt in it. Lamas always drink butter-tea. For mode of preparation see p. 132.

† "Draba" is a general appellation for all inmates of monasteries, whether they have taken orders or not.

behind ; and, although the gegen has many valuables, I have taken nothing belonging to him. Still, I considered it prudent to take the road to Gyangtse at once.

A woman working in the fields pointed out the road and, after walking all day, towards evening I came upon a muleman pitching camp. I told him where I had come from and that I wanted to go to my uncle, who lived at Gangtog in Sikhim. He enquired my uncle's name and I told him that he was generally called Balu, a nickname meaning "funny man." He said that he knew Balu very well and promised to take me to him : he had lately heard that he was sick. He told me to give my bag of tsamba to his servant and he would look after me and let me ride a mule. He had a caravan of thirty or forty mules, and was on his way home to Chumbi from Lhasa, where he had been trading Indian for Lhasa goods. We took more than twenty days to get to Chumbi, as the mules were very slow. Ordinarily one can walk it in fourteen days ; Lhasa to Gyangtse is seven days, Gyangtse to Pari Dzong five days, and Pari to Chumbi two days. When we got to Chumbi, the muleman said that he must rest a few days and I could stay with him ; or, if I wished to go on at once, he would send me with others going that way and give me a letter to Balu. I stayed with him in Chumbi, and after a few days he took me to Gangtog. There I learned that my uncle had died many days before.

At Gangtog is the palace of the Maharajah of Sikhim. It is built on the top of a mountain, and round the palace are the residences of the Maharajah's ministers, who are called Kaji. It was in one of these that my uncle had lived, going every day to the palace on business. A British officer lived in Gangtog, an old gentleman whose name I never heard: he was called the burra sahib.* There is no town, only a small bazaar. Balu's wife had died two or three years before, and there was an only child, a boy of eight or nine years of age, who was being looked after by my uncle's friends. Balu had told them all about his family in Kam,† and they asked me questions about them, and told me that my father's name was Sherap,‡ which means "Wisdom." One of the kajis, who had been a friend of my uncle, took me to live with him until he considered what should be done: and after a month or two he sent me and my brother§ to a little school of about a dozen boys in the palace. A very good lama from Drashilhunbo was our gegen.

My second hot season came round, and as, being from Tibet, I had not stood the first summer in Gangtog very well, my brother and I were sent to Rumdig monastery, which is on a very high mountain not far from Gangtog.|| We had been there two weeks when my face broke out in a rash. It happened that an American missionary, Cheddard by name, had come to camp on the mountain, so I went to see him; he put some medicine on my face and gave me some

* Presumably Mr. Claud White, the first British Political Officer appointed to Sikhim. Sir Charles Bell, who succeeded him, states that he was regarded with affection and respect by all classes of the population.—*Bell*, p. 92.

† "Kam" is a general name for Eastern Tibet.

‡ Father's name. "Family names are unknown in Tibet, and children are spoken of as of such and such a woman; hardly ever is the father's name mentioned." *Rock.: L. of L.*, p. 213.

§ "Brother"—I have let this word stand throughout the text. As Rockhill points out (*ibid.* note), the Tibetan language has no word to express "cousin."

|| Sir Charles Bell informs me that, although situated on the top of a ridge across the Rongnye Valley, Rumdig is really two or three hundred feet lower than Gangtog.

to take home with me. He said, "This is a small sickness ; but your soul is very sick ; it will be more difficult to cure." Thinking he meant that I had some serious ailment in my inside, I assured him that it was not so, that my body was very strong. But he said that I was mistaken, and advised me to think it out. He gave me a little book and said : "Read this ; then you will know." My face was cured in a week, and I read the book, which was the "Gospel according to St. John" in Tibetan. Much of it seemed very wonderful, but a great deal of it I could not understand. The book was bound very beautifully and I kept it for a long time.

I was in Gangtog one year and a half, and I wanted very much to learn English and Hindustani, which they did not teach in the little school in the palace. Having heard that the Swedish Mission near Darjeeling had a school where they taught these languages, and also Tibetan, free of charge, I left my brother behind in Gangtog and went to Darjeeling, a three days' journey, travelling in company with some fruit-sellers. At the Mission I found that the teacher of Tibetan was a lama from Dartsendo, and he offered to take me in and to speak to Miss Kronquist, the head of the Mission. He arranged things so that I stayed at his house, and the Mission ladies gave me meals. I took my father's name, Sherap, and dropped Dorje Zödba. The lama was broadminded and, although a good Buddhist, told me that all religions were good. At the school they taught me the gospels, Tibetan, English, Hindustani, carpentry, and embroidery. I am still very good at embroidering silk flowers on table-cloths. Very near the Mission was a little lamasery called Ghoom, where was a Geshi,* very knowledgeful, and he liked to teach me Buddhist doctrine. I went to him for an hour or half-an-hour every day. But Buddhism was too difficult for me ; Christianity was more easy to understand.

After I had been in the Mission a little over three years, there came to Darjeeling from Dsogchen in Derge, a lama called Pedma Rinchen, who was making the pilgrimage to the temple at Budhgaya, not far from Benares. I wanted very badly to go with him, but had no money for the railway journey. Finally he promised to take me and, as a "good work,"† to pay my fare. The Mission was angry at my wishing to go off with him, but I no care. This pilgrimage to Budhgaya was only the first of many which I made in company with Pedma Rinchen. Altogether our pilgrimages lasted about two years‡ and I shall tell you all we saw, but first of all I must tell you how I came to be here in Dartsendo.

When I returned from my pilgrimages with Pedma Rinchen, my brother was still living in Gangtog, and I took him to the Mission. I found that Miss Kronquist had left, and Miss Haskennen had taken her place. The lama from Dartsendo was still there, and my brother and I were allowed to live in the Mission. I remained for two and a half years, studying the same languages as before, and then I was baptised by the name of Paul. There being no man in the Mission at that time, the

* A "Geshi" is a draba who has taken a degree ; it may be translated "B.D."

† "Good works."—For each good work in this life the departed spirit, when appearing before the judgment-seat of the King of Hell, receives a white pebble in the scale to weigh against the black pebbles representing his sins.

‡ Apparently 1903–5.

ceremony was performed by a Bengalese called Moses, who had a little chapel of his own at Kurhsiang and kept a shoemaker's and also a tailor's shop. For a time I helped him in his business and in his chapel, receiving food and clothes but no wages; however, after about a year, I thought "no good doing this till I am old," and, as I had spent all my money, I went to Darjeeling to look for a job. Miss Ferguson, of the Tibetan Pioneer Mission, employed me to manage the marketing and to preach on Sundays, and I stayed there until she went home to Glasgow two years later. Then a Chinese friend in Calcutta advised me of a situation which was vacant there. The Asiatic Society of Bengal had a Kangjur which was badly printed, and they wanted someone to revise the text.* I went to Calcutta and obtained this appointment, and it occupied my time for almost two years.

While I was thus employed, the Chinese revolution broke out, and the Chinese garrison was driven out of Tibet into India.† The escaping troops received from the Indian Government a free passage by railway to Calcutta. One of their officers, Ma Chi-fu, came to live with me and, being like the rest without money, borrowed over 300 rupees. Half a month later he told me that the Indian Government was going to repatriate them all, and begged me to go with them as interpreter, saying that my salary would be paid and my loan

* "Kangjur": the Tibetan canon, consisting of 108 volumes containing 40–50,000 leaves.

† This was in 1912. Lhasa had been occupied by Chinese troops early in 1910, when the Dalai Lama fled to Darjeeling. Towards the end of 1912, by which time all Chinese troops had left the country, he was recognised by the Republican Government as head of the Lamaist Church.—*Teichman*, pp. 15–17.

returned so soon as they reached Shanghai. Now, it had so happened that the year before two Mongolian lama officials passed through Calcutta from Lhasa on their way back to Peking, and on the strength of my knowledge of Hindustani and English as well as Tibetan, had promised me remunerative employment in Peking if I would go there. They gave me papers of recommendation. I thought this a good chance to go to China, so accompanied Ma and the rest ; but when we got to Shanghai they declared themselves unable to pay me because, they explained, they were Szechuanese and the Shanghai people did not know them ; if I would only continue with them until they reached Chengtu they would pay me there without fail. It seemed to me to be useless to go on to Peking, as the Manchu Government had disappeared, and, on the other hand, if I went to Chêngtu, I should have a chance of revisiting my native place, of which I had very dim memories. So I went with them.

At Ichang my eyes became very bad, and I was almost blind. At Padung, near Kueifu, my companions told me to wait in the inn while they arranged about a passage to Chungking. I waited some time and then on making enquiries learned that they had gone off without me ; my boxes also had disappeared, and I discovered them lying empty by the river side. I had only one dollar in my pocket and could not get anyone to believe my story, as I was not very fluent in Chinese, and had difficulty in explaining what had happened. Then I was taken to the magistrate, who detained me on suspicion for seven days, when, fortunately, a Tibetan boy was found to interpret for me. The upshot was that the magistrate agreed to send me as far as Kueifu, but could not do more. My eyes were now a little better, and when we reached Kueifu, I persuaded the boatmen for 1,000 cash to take me on to Wanhsien.*

At Wanhsien I met Messrs. Darlington and Snow, of the China Inland Mission, who helped me greatly with medicine and food. I stayed there for one month, until Mr. Sörensen of the same Mission arrived on his way to Dartsendo. He spoke and read Tibetan very well, and offered to take me with him. So I came here, and was pundit to Mr. Sörensen, and preached and translated many gospels and tracts, and also wrote tracts myself.

In 1913 I married a Tibetan lady, and had four boys and one girl. She died a year ago, and I have since married a lady who is half Tibetan and half Chinese. I also started a business here, exporting musk to Shanghai, but trade has been very bad for some time now, owing to the continual fighting in Szechuan. The only travelling I have done has been two trips into Derge in connection with the purchase of Tibetan books.

There are in Tibet three presses where they print the Kangjur, a copy of which Mr. Sörensen wished to obtain. One is at Nartang† in Tsang, one at Litang in Kam, and one at Derge Gonchen. The Litang press was wrecked by Chinese at the beginning of the Republic, but I understand that two or three years ago Lhasa acquired a printing-press of its own. The presses at Drashilhunbo, Rongbatsa, and other places do not print the Kangjur, only small books.

* In Szechuan "cash" generally average over 3,000 to the Mexican dollar. 1,000 cash are about equivalent to 8d.

† Nartang is not far from Drashilhunbo, the capital of the province of Tsang. Tsang and U (capital—Lhasa) together form Tibet proper.

The Derge press produces the best and clearest type, but when, three years after my arrival in Dartsendo, Mr. Sörensen and myself visited it, printing had temporarily stopped. The characters in the Derge Kangjur are printed in red, the ink coming from Shen Chou Hsien,* in Hunan, and they were at that time unable to procure it.

Our journey to Derge took us through Rongbatsa,† where I enquired about my relatives. At first no one remembered the name, but by and by two or three women called on us, one of whom shook hands with me in the foreign fashion, and, bursting into tears, said that she was my sister ; she invited Mr. Sorensen and myself to go to her house next day for milk and bread. There we met many of my mother's friends, who brought presents of dried meat, butter, tsamba, beer, wolf-skins, rupees, and kadas‡ for me. We remained in Rongbatsa in a wealthy Tibetan merchant's house for three days, and then went on to Yilhung, in the Derge nomad country, to see my brother. We stayed in the Yilhung official's house, while I sent a message to my brother, who was living as hermit in a snow mountain. He came in next morning with two drabas, bringing presents of sour milk, meat, sweet potatoes, butter, and cheese, but he would not come under the roof, as it was against his vow to do so. He pitched two tents outside and we went there to talk. He was very happy to see me, saying that he had thought

* Shen Chou Hsien, in Hunan, is noted for its cinnabar, which is used in the manufacture of vermilion ink.—cf. Williams' *Middle Kingdom*, II, p. 62.

† From Dartsendo to Rongbatsa is about 240 miles in a north-westerly direction.

‡ Kada is a scarf of silk or muslin, most commonly used in making ceremonial calls or as presents.

I was dead and that I appeared like one resurrected. He enquired about Balu, and I told him that he was dead, and of his son, and many things we talked of all that night. Then he gave me some sheepskins to sleep on in the tent, but they smelt so strong that I could not stand them and went back to the official's house. In the morning he sent for me and asked why I had gone away. I could not tell him of the sheepskins, and he said, "You don't like me; also you are Christian, it is too bad. You must change religion and come with me; I give you plenty yak and cattle." But I told him I could not change religion, must be Christian. "Of course I will love you and will send letters from Dartsendo, but I cannot live with you; you are lama, and I got wife and children."

We stayed at Yilhung for four days and then set out for Derge Gonchen. There are three great lamaseries in Derge, their names in order of importance being Dsogchen, Gartog, and Beyü, all of the Nyima sect. Nyima has three sub-sects—Chakchen, Dsogchen, and Wumachen; these are Mahayana, but some other sub-sects are slightly Hinayana. We stopped at the Dsogchen Monastery, where are some 1,000 drabas under the Dsogchen Rinboche Pedma Riktsin. My friend, Pedma Rinchen, who happened to be in Dsogchen, called on us. He was looking old. He was very glad to see me, and we told each other all that had happened since we parted. He had stayed at Gyangtse for four years before returning to Dsogchen, and was now thinking of making a pilgrimage to Koko Nor to see the great lamasery there, and the lake which has an impress of Pedma Sambhava's hand. He did not say anything about my having become Christian. A year or two later, passing through Dsogchen a second time, on my way to Derge, I enquired for Pedma Rinchen, and learned that he was away in Koko Nor.

CHAPTER III

MAN AND THE UNIVERSE.

Drasrinmo and the Monkey—Scriptural story of the same—Lamaist Account of Creation—The Wish-granting Tree, and the war between Lha and Lhamayin—The Six Gati—Kalpas, and the approach of the Tselojuba—The Nag country.

OLD folk in Tibet believe that men are descended from Drasrinmo and a monkey, who lived in a cave on Gönbori, the Gönbo's Mountain, south-east of Lhasa. Near Gönbori is Tsetang, which gets its name, meaning "Playground," from the fact that their offspring played there. These latter were so numerous and diverse in character—beasts, birds, fishes, creeping things, and man—that in course of time the children of men migrated to Mount K'unlun, down whose four sides flowed four great rivers issuing from the mouths of a horse, an elephant, a lion, and a peacock; and following these several streams, they became widely separated and divergent in race. The Horse River, Dacho Kabab, flowed east past Gönbori; the Elephant River, Langjen Kabab, north to Mongolia; the Lion River, Singjen Kabab, west to Ladak; and the Peacock River, Magjia Kabab, south through Burong to India.* The appetite of

* The introduction of the name K'unlun shows influence of Chinese, who have a similar legend associated with that sacred mountain from which they believe they originated. But the Mount Meru or Sumeru of the Indian myth, in Tibetan Rirab, is identified by Indians as Mount Kailas, called by Tibetans Gangar Dise or Gang Rinboche. The four rivers, which also figure in the Indian story, are the Tsangbo or Bramaputra (Horse), the Sutlej (Elephant), the Indus (Lion), and the Gogra (Peacock). These all rise in the neighbourhood of Dise, and the holy Lake Mapam or Manasarovara. Sven Hedin places the sources of the Tsangbo and the Sutlej on the northern flank of the Himalayas (East of L. Manasarovara), and that of the Indus to the north of the western Trans-Himalaya Range (North of Mount Kailas).—See *Trans-Himalaya, passim.*

Tibetans for raw flesh is attributed to their demonic origin; they ascribe the wisdom of men to their descent from the monkey.

Of the intermarriage of the first offspring implied in this account nothing is said. Incest is abhorred in Tibet: not only are those guilty of it severely punished after death, but their crime brings bad luck to all their neighbours: Tibetans of the same blood do not intermarry. There is no tradition of a flood which might have driven the people to take refuge on the mountain, although it is true that, when Drasrinmo and her mate lived on Gönbori, all the country round what is now Lhasa was under water, with the exception of the rocky hill on which afterwards the Potala was built.*

The story, as given by Sönam Yungdrung, secretary at the Commissioner's yamen, who is a good scholar and believer in the Bön creed, is as follows: "About twenty days' journey south-east of Lhasa is a monastery called Gombo Bönri, the Monastery of Mount Bön, among whose rocks is a cave known as the Demoness's Cave, Srinmotadsa; and in the beginning, before other life existed in Tibet, the cave was inhabited by a demoness, Drasrinmo. At this time Janrezig, the Merciful One, bethought himself in Potala† that he would make a world of men. Accordingly he sent a Bodhisattva in the form of a monkey to earth, saying to him: 'Go to Srinmotadsa and there meditate on how to create a living world.'

* "The name Lhasa is properly restricted to the great temple (Jo-wo-Kang). Srongtsangampo appears to have been the founder of the city now generally known to Europeans as Lhasa. It is recorded that (it was originally) a village named Rasa which, on account of the temple he erected, was altered to Lha-sa, or God's Place."—*Wadd.*

† Potala: the mythical Indian residence of Avalokita (Janrezig), from which the palace at Lhasa gets its name.

Obedient to this command, the Bodhisattva descended and commenced his meditations in the cave of the rock-demoness; but he had no success, owing to being plagued by her interruptions. Eventually he returned to Potala and represented to Janrezig that his meditations were fruitless, as the creature in the cave was always teasing him for something. Janrezig replied that he must return to the cave and do all that Drasrinmo wished.

"After the monkey had lived with Drasrinmo in the cave for some time, the offspring—in the form of beasts, birds, fishes, insects, and man—were so numerous that the monkey was unable to find food for them all, and was obliged again to go to Potala and inform Janrezig of the circumstances, saying that without help his children would all die of hunger. Janrezig then gave him the seed of five kinds of grain, which he was to scatter on the earth; he need not labour at tilling the ground or tending the crops: they would spring up of themselves and produce all that would be required for food and clothing. The grain was for the use of mankind only, whom he must carefully cherish, but the beasts must be sent away to roam abroad and forage for food. And so it came about that the animals went into the forests and the mountains and the rivers and underneath the earth, while the children of men fed on grain and clothed themselves."

The above story is from the sacred books, and the same informant tells of the creation of the universe as follows: "In the beginning the universe was void, and there existed only the two spirits, Adi-Buddha and his consort, Chijam Jelmo. Meditating on the work of creation, Adi-Buddha set as the foundations of the world two dorjes crossed.* Then, revolving ideas in his mind, he created successively the elements: fire, water, wind, and earth; and from these he constructed the four great worlds which he placed at the four points of the compass, each with two satellites; and in the centre, separated from the four worlds by seven seas and seven mountain ranges, he placed the great mountain, Rijel Lhunbo or Rirab. The four worlds are:—

Lüpag, the eastern world, white and crescent-shaped;
Dsambuling, southern world, blue and triangular;
Balangjö, western world, red and round; and
Draminyen, northern world, green and square.

The inhabitants of each have faces of the same shape as the world they live in. Dsambuling is our own world. Half-way up Mount Rirab, the centre of the universe, is a wish-granting tree, called Bagsamshing, so tall that, while its roots are in the country of the Lhamayin, its top is in that of the Lha. And above Rirab are the thirty-three heavens, the highest of which is the abode of Adi-Buddha.

"The conventional way of representing the creation of the universe by Adi-Buddha shows him with a revolving wheel on his breast. As the wheel turns, the mystic symbol AH first comes uppermost, creating the dorjes; with a further turn the symbol MAN appears, creating fire; then successively the symbols RAM, YAM, KAM, creating water, wind, and earth respectively. Having made all these, Adi-Buddha, from out of his eyes, extracted the Sun and the Moon, the former composed of fire-

* The "dorje" (vajra) corresponds to the thunderbolt of Jove. Those used in the foundation of the world were made of a substance called "blue air" of adamantine strength.—*Wadd.*, p. 77.

crystal, and the latter of water-crystal, and he also made the eight planets and the stars. Last of all, a white ray emanated from him, and a red one from his consort, which united and produced life in the universe."

Sönam Yungdrung holds that the explanation of the origin of life given in this account is not irreconcilable with the story of the descent of man from a monkey. When Adi-Buddha created life, he disregarded Tibet, where life was introduced later through the agency of Janrezig, in the manner described.

As already mentioned, below the country of the Lha, on the lower slopes of Mount Rirab, is the country of the Lhamayin, pugnacious people of hot temper who are always warring on the Lha because they pluck the fruit of the tree Bagsamshing. Many of the Lhamayin are wounded and die, but in the Lha country is a spring of water, called Dsenjurtsel, to which the Kings of the Lha, Tsangba and Jeljin, take Lha warriors that are wounded, and these, drinking of it, are soon made well. At one time, when a Lhamayin was killed, many hundred more sprang from his blood. Consequently the Lha were so hard pressed in battle that their king called on Adi-Buddha to help him. His consort heard the appeal and came down in person ; and from the king she received a mule as charger, with saddle of human skin, and bridle and reins of serpents. Having defeated the Lhamayin she drank the blood of the slain, using a human skull as cup, and by doing so put an end for ever to their power of raising soldiers from the blood of the dead. Thereafter she was always worshipped as a Lhamo, and goddess of war under the names Lhamo Magzorma and Baldan Lhamo. She is the deity of whom the late Queen Victoria was said to be a reincarnation.*

The Lha and Lhamayin are only two out of the six classes of sentient beings, the other four being Man, the Animals, the Yidag, and the sufferers in Hell. The six Gati inhabited by these beings are generally spoken of as real and separate countries, and are actually represented as such in pictures of the Wheel of Life. But, except for the Lha and Lhamayin, who live on Mount Rirab and are invisible, they exist in fact together and mingle with each other, and we see them every day in our own world. We must all, when we die, according to the doctrine of transmigration, appear before the King of Hell, who after reviewing our good and bad deeds in this world will decide in which of the Gati we are to spend our next life. The three first Gati, those of Lha, Lhamayin, and Man, are regarded as good ; the other three bad.

Time is measured by kalpas, ages. Sacred books say that in olden times men lived for 10,000 years, but, as it grows more sinful, each generation has a shorter life. Not so very long ago men lived normally for 100 years, but they seldom do so now. Thirty

* "In her second attitude, or milder aspect, she is seated on a mule which she guides with a bridle of snakes, holding an umbrella of peacocks' feathers over her head. The fact that in her second aspect the goddess is riding her mule, seated sideways as an European lady, has given currency to a curious idea which deserves to be mentioned. Many years ago certain pictures from the *Illustrated London News*, in which Queen Victoria was shown in early life sitting on horseback to review the troops, found their way into Thibet. As the great Empress of India was commonly accounted in Thibet as a personage warlike as well as of far-reaching sway, those pictures started the notion that Queen Victoria was an incarnation of Goddess Baldan Lhamo. (See *Ramsay's Western Tibetan Dictionary*.) And so in Thibet at the present day, it is always held. . . . It was the Empress Katharine of Russia that set going the Drölma incarnations on the Russian throne."—*Sandberg*, p. 211.

years ago the marriage age was 20 to 22; now it is 16 to 20, and people are becoming old at 30 or 35, which used to be the prime of life. By and by the time will come when they will marry at 5 and die at 10 years of age; that is what is known as the Tselojuba period, the end of the kalpa, when Maitreya will appear. Maitreya is very large and portly, and all the little people will go to him and enquire how it is that he is so big, and he will answer that it is by doing "good works"; if they followed his example, they would be like him.* So, attending to this, the small people will begin to live longer; and that will be the beginning of a new kalpa.

A more simple theory of the universe than that described above divides it into three regions: Heaven (Nam), Earth (Sa), and the Serpent Kingdom (Lu; Skt. Nag). Man cannot see the Nag country: it is underneath the earth: but thence come all creatures that live in water—worms, frogs, fishes, serpents, dragons; and the king of this region, the Nagrajah, is half-man and half-serpent, only the upper half of his body being human. From his watery kingdom he supplies rain to heaven, and it is to him that the lamas pray when rain is wanted. The Nagrajah sleeps during winter, and Tibetans cannot worship him then, but by consulting the sacred books they know the exact dates of the beginning and end of his hibernating period. Old folk say that rain is dragon's milk. The belief (not shared by lamas) is that the Nagrajah sends a pair of dragons (druk) up to heaven and, if they have offspring, both are so happy that they rush round playing. Should the

* Maitreya, the coming Buddha, in Tib. Jamba. Statues of him are often of colossal height, 70 to 80 feet, or more.

mother dragon have an excess of milk, it pours down in the shape of rain ; while the noise that seems to come from the rain is really caused by the dragons rushing round.*

* In China also the dragon sends rain : relic of widespread serpent worship. According to Waddell, the worship of dragons or nagas is a special feature of the Bön religion.

CHAPTER IV

SOME RELIGIOUS CUSTOMS.

The private chapel—The Chöba—Morning and Evening Prayers—Om-Mani-Pedme-Hum—Ma Dra Mu Ye Sa Le Du—The good mind—Mani—Ladse—Prayer Wheels—Chöden—"Beating the Drum"—New Year observances: burning the dorma: the family treasure chest: the luck arrow: the meal-throwing—Fêtes to the Zhidag—Circumambulating mountains—The Pilgrimage to Lhasa—Jangchaba ascetics—Lama Pilgrimages.

NEXT to the living room in almost every Tibetan house, excepting the very humble, is a room reserved as a chapel, and known as the chökang, or house of offerings. Those who can afford it employ a lama, amchö, to recite the scriptures there every day: he is in charge of the chökang and holds the key, keeps the place clean, and renews the offering-water daily. The chökang is not much used by the family, who visit it only occasionally to kotow to the chöjong, leaving their religious duties largely to the care of the amchö, where there is one, or to outside lamas. But its furnishings are so common all over the country, being found regularly even in the tents of the nomads, and I shall refer so frequently to the chöba, with its dorma and other accessories, that it will be well at once to give a description of the usual equipment of the chökang.

Against the wall farthest from the door are three long, narrow tables, or standing shelves, set one above the other, on which are placed the offerings, chöba—the principal feature of the room. The composition of the chöba varies with the occasion: one kind is used at baptismal services, another at services for sickness, and so on; but for general purposes the chöba is the same, modified only according to the wealth of the household. As commonly used, the word includes both altar and offering. The highest table, which is also the shortest, supports a row of what are called "dorma." Shaped more or less like vases or bottles,* the dorma are made of tsamba and are usually decorated with two discs of butter, having a red spot in the centre, one disc in the place where a label would be, the other near the top of the neck. The middle one of the row is sometimes of considerable size, made of wood smeared over with butter, and not infrequently surmounted by a wooden framework coated with white or black-coloured butter and ornamented with designs of the "eight lucky signs,"† also in butter. The second table holds the butter lamps, silver or brass goblets with a small hole in which stands a wick of plaited cotton thread or of cotton wool wrapped round a splinter of bamboo. Filled with butter and with the wicks alight the lamps are in effect candles, and their number need be limited only by the size of the table or altar. The third and lowest altar holds the offering bowls, of which there must be at least seven, but there may be a hundred. Of the seven, two contain water and the others a flower, a stick of incense, a butter lamp, saffron water, and tsamba respectively. Saffron (kachishakam or dri-sang)—"the Tibetan red flower" as the Chinese call

* Or "Indian clubs."

† "The Eight Auspicious Symbols" (drashi-da-je) are: The Wheel, Double Swastika, Water Vase, Two Golden Fish, Conch-shell, Lotus, Victorious Banner, and Umbrella.

it—is regarded as a great purifier, and is "blest of Buddha." On great occasions, in the middle of the row, is set a "mendel," a sort of three-tiered cake of tsamba or rice, representing Mount Rirab, the central point of the four worlds, which themselves are symbolised by grains of barley, precious stones, and metals, the whole being intended as an offering of the Universe. Usually a vase of flowers is placed at either end of this row, and on the floor in front is a brazier in which juniper is burned, its aromatic fragrance being well known to please the unseen powers. On the wall behind the chöba is a wooden structure containing idols, flanked on either side by shelves holding sacred books*; and along each of the side walls are pictures of Buddhas, Chöjong, and saints, in front of which smaller chöba may be placed. Every evening for an hour or two lamas come and recite the scriptures, or "beat the drum," as the service is commonly called, and clash their cymbals to remind the Chöjong of the needs of the family and the prayers it has offered.

In saying that the Tibetan family leaves its religious duties largely in the hands of lamas, I would not imply that it entirely neglects religious observances itself: far from it. The services performed by the lamas are of a ceremonial kind, not within the competence, according to prevailing belief, of laymen.† On rising each morning the Tibetan prays first to Janrezig, the Merciful One, then to the Three Holy Ones, and finally to the canonised lamas; which done, he mounts to the roof,

* The sacred books are worshipped as embodying Buddha's Law, the second of "The Three Holy Ones."

† There is a Tibetan saying: "Without a Lama in front, there is no approach to God."

and in the mud stove there burns juniper to the defenders of the faith, making offerings of butter, tea, and tsamba, and calling on Chöjong and Zhidag by name. Only then does he commence his working day and break his fast. So in the evening: the family sits round the floor, in the kitchen or living room, reciting from memory the sacred books. Afterwards, on going to their respective couches, each prays to the Three Holy Ones, kneeling three times while doing so. These prayers differ little from those of a devout Christian; they give thanks for protection during the past day; ask forgiveness for the day's sins; and pray for protection during the coming night. They pray also to Janrezig and the canonised lamas, using the ordinary rosary of 108 beads, and repeating Om-Mani-Pedme-Hum as they tell off each bead, praying that their dead parents and all other dead be cleansed from sin (digba dagbar shog), that is, that they go to Dewajen (Sukhavati); and sometimes the devotee prays that his happiness be transferred to the rest of mankind and the sorrows of other men be placed on his head alone. The idea that the dead may go to Dewajen is of course not pure Buddhism, but the lamas say that this escape from transmigration is possible. Not so long ago the Geluba sect, through the Drashilhunbo lama, started a belief that all good Tibetans will go not to Sukhavati but to Shambhala (Tib. Dejün), the Northern Paradise, and this creed is now accepted by those of the Geluba faith.

The Three Holy Ones just mentioned, to whom prayer is daily offered, are Buddha, Buddha's Word, and the Priesthood; in Sanskrit Buddha, Dharma and Sanggha. The three extra beads seen on rosaries are symbolical of the Holy Three.

Om-Mani-Pedme-Hum (Pedme being pronounced Beme) was unknown in Tibet until Thonmi Sambota brought it with the Buddhistic doctrines from India. In India it was understood to mean : "Oh, the Jewel in the Lotus," the Jewel being Avalokitesvara (Janrezig). Sambota's patron, the King Songdsengombo, was recognised as a reincarnation of Janrezig, who now through the King gave the formula a new significance, according to which the utterance of these six syllables was a prayer that the denizens of the six Gati should be purified of sin, released from the bonds of metempsychosis, and allowed to go to Dewajen. The utterance of the syllable Om was a prayer to free the Lha, of Ma to free the Lhamayin, of Ni, to free Man ; Ped, the Animals ; Me, the Yidag ; and Hum, the unfortunates in Hell. That this interpretation was actually recognised as far back as the time of Songdsengombo is proved by the fact that it is so given in the Manekabum, which was written during the lifetime of that King.*

The Bön religion has a similar prayer, which runs : Ma Dra Mu Ye Sa Le Du, and which the

* Unfortunately for the soundness of this argument, no good evidence exists to show that the Manekabum dates back to the seventh century. Rockhill ascribes it " in all likelihood " to the fifteenth, after the establishment of the Lhasa pontificate by Tsongkaba ; and he finds the earliest reference to the Mani in the twelfth century. Extracts which he gives in translation from the Manekabum, to illustrate the story of the origin of the Mani formula, tell us that on the intercession of Janrezig, Obame allowed the utterance of the six syllables to close the gates of rebirth ; and the Mani, as the prayer is colloquially called in Tibet, is an invocation to Janrezig, whose one great self-imposed mission is the salvation of all living creatures from the miseries incident to sentient existence, that he will, hearing it, ever keep the world in mind.—See *Land of the Lamas*, Supp., note 2. A cat, when purring, is said to be " telling its beads," from the resemblance of the sound to the muttered repetition of the Mani formula. Chinese cats also " tell their beads " (nien Fo).

interpreter at the Commissioner's yamen, himself a follower of the Bön system, says was introduced into Tibet by Shenrab, the founder of the Black Bön or Bön Nag. Its original significance was lost when the Black Bön, with its human sacrifices and diabolical rites, was completely extirpated by King Trisongdedsen, and it now bears the same interpretation as the Lamaist Mani prayer, that interpretation having been adopted by the present White Bön or Bön Gar. The first syllable Ma is a prayer that the sins of the founder of the Bön religion be purified; Dra, those of the inhabitants of Hell; Mu, of the Yidag; Ye, of the Animals; Sa, of Man; Le, of the Lhamayin; and Du, of the Lha. He adds that Shenrab was born at Ormolungring, in Persia, and, like Buddha, from the side of his mother's breast.*

From the account just given you might think that Tibetans, being much given to prayer, are a pious, good people, but this does not necessarily follow. For even robbers use the prayer-wheel and the rosary; but they thrust them in the breast of their sheepskin when a rich man appears on the road, and handle sword and gun instead, their hearts not being clean. It is the mind that matters. Hence the saying:—

> Ka Yag Mo Mani Dön Ba Le
> Sem Gang Gar Ka Rog Ded Na Ga

meaning,

> Repetition of Mani by the mouth is vain;
> Better a good mind than fair words.

* Shenrab is by some identified with the Chinese philosopher Laotzu, who flourished in the 6th or 7th centuries B.C. Jaeschke (*Dict.*, p. 132) mentions that Buddhas born on the earth are not born from the womb, but from the side, near the heart. Rhys Davids (p. 183, footnote) quotes St. Jerome: "It is handed down as a tradition among the Gymnosophists of India that Buddha, the founder of their system, was brought forth by a virgin from her side."

And again,

Sam Ba Zang Na Sa Dang Lam Yang Zang
Sam Ba Ngan Na Sa Dang Lam Yang Ngan

that is,

If the mind is good, all the world is good ;
If the mind is bad, all the world is bad.

Perhaps it is an idea like the one expressed in these last lines that has given rise to the opinion among some foreigners that Tibetans believe a virtuous man will always be favoured by Nature : that the sun will always shine when he travels and the wind and rain spare him. It is not so. If it rains, blows, or snows on the road, the right-minded man will regard the storm as a temporary ill that can be remedied by a change of clothing when he reaches his destination. He does not allow his mind to be affected by his environment. There is nothing more in it than that. So in small matters : if a servant breaks a plate, or brings in a lamp that smokes, as happened just now, the big man is not disturbed by the incident, for it was not done on purpose* ; smashing a plate in a fit of temper is another thing : it argues that the mind is bad.

However, in spite of their appreciation of the value of a good mind, the fact is that mechanical prayer is an obsession with Tibetans. If one's father or other near relative dies, filial respect calls for the erection of what is called a "mani," the nucleus of which is a seat made of stone or mud which is concealed under a pile of slabs inscribed with the mani formula, the whole crowned with

* Fortunately for my reputation I had decided to postpone chiding the careless rascal until after Sherap had gone.

prayer-flags.* Sometimes it is cairn-shaped, at other times you see it in the form of a long wall of such slabs with a "chöden," or offering-holder, at either end of it, dividing the roadway bilaterally; and if you wish to avoid being sacrilegious, you will, in travelling, always keep such mani on your right hand—unless you are of the Bön creed, in which case you will keep them on the left. These mani are intended to give an opportunity to devout persons to perform "good works" by circumambulating them, and so ensuring transit of the deceased to Dewajen. But some mani, on a mountain side, or near a river, have been erected with the object, not of providing opportunities for "good works," but of placating the angry spirit of one who has died a violent death in these lonely spots.

Not unlike the mani in appearance, although without the inscriptions, are the stone cairns called "ladse," erected on mountain tops to propitiate the mountain spirits (Zhidag), and incidentally point the way to travellers, who in passing are careful to add a stone or a prayer-flag to the pile. Usually the flag bears a crude picture of the "Lung Da," wind horse, with the three jewels on its saddle; or else the names of Vajrapan, Manjusri, and Avalokitesvara, whose aid is thus invoked.

But it is with the Wheel (Korlo) that mechanical prayer is chiefly associated. Prayer-wheels are of many varieties, but have one feature in common, namely, a drum or cylinder with the prayer inscribed on the outside in Tibetan or Sanskrit, and printed many thousand times on paper

* "Such monuments are called in both Mongol and Chinese Obo—a Mongolised Tibetan word."—*Rock., L. of L.*, p. 127.

in the inside. It is turned from right to left; and, passing through the porticos of lamaseries, one revolves a row of them by drawing one's right hand along their surface without pausing in one's walk; followers of the Bön of course revolve them in the opposite direction. In the small hand-wheel, "Lagkor," the cylinder is fixed on a short wooden handle. Large prayer drums are sometimes turned by a crank worked by hand. The table wheel is simply a drum, and is set going by giving a twist to the knob on the top of the axle. The water prayer wheel, "Chukor," sometimes of great size, is suspended over a stream, the end of its axle carrying a wooden wheel which, turned by the stream, turns the great barrel round with it. The wind wheel, "Lungkor," is hung from a pole, and is revolved by means of an arrangement of cups that catch the breeze. Fire wheels, "Mekor," are turned by hot air from butter lamps.

In speaking of the mani wall, I mentioned a kind of monument the name of which, like chöba, dorma, and so on, will frequently recur. The "chöden" assumes a multitude of forms, but essentially consists of a small, square, stone chamber, on top of which is a large globe or urn, surmounted by a tall cone, the whole perhaps ten to twenty feet high. The square chamber rests on three plinths, the abodes of the Naga, of Man, and of the Lhamayin. The chamber holds the offerings, which consist usually of "tsa-tsa," or miniature chödens of mud, samples of gold, silver, copper, iron, shells, coral, barley, wheat, peas, silk of five colours, and sometimes prayer-books. Between this chamber and the globe are three more plinths, the lowest being the abode of Lha, and the highest of Adi-Buddha; I forget what the middle one represents. The globe is supposed to hold Buddha's doctrines; and the cone above it, divided into thirteen segments, represents Buddha's thirteen sutras. On the peak of the cone are models of the sun and moon, emblematic of the light introduced by the Buddhistic teachings, from which springs a flame symbolical of the fire with which they warm the devotee. Such are the chödens usually seen on mani walls and near lamaseries.*

Chödens are not invariably offering-holders. Some are designed to repress the activities of evil spirits, others as receptacles for the remains of saints, of which latter kind the famous examples in Nepal measure from one to two hundred feet in height. Chödens of a temporary character are also erected for cremation purposes.

The fondness of Tibetans for ceremonial observances is indicated by the fact that every third or fourth day is marked on the calendar for some special "beating of the drum." On the 3rd, 13th, and 23rd of each moon is held the luck-bringing ceremony of "Lhasang," for which lamas are called, who burn incense and juniper, and offer tea, wine, and barley in the chökang, after which they go up on the roof and repeat the service there, in order to propitiate the evil spirits known as Zhidag. The Lhasang, with its accompaniment of drums and cymbals, must be over by mid-day. Against danger

* Many of the Lamaist Caityas (or Chödens) are, like those of the Japanese, symbolic of the five elements into which a body is resolved upon death; thus, the lowest section, a solid rectangular block, typifies the solidity of the *earth*; above it *water* is represented by a globe; *fire* by a triangular tongue; *air* by a crescent—the inverted vault of the sky; and *ether* by an acumigated circle, the tapering into space.—*Wadd.*, p. 263.

from sickness and violence from robbers, etc., the goddess Drölma is invoked on the 8th and 18th, when four or eight lamas are engaged, with drums, bells, and cymbals, and with offerings of tea and tsamba, to enlist her protection. And again, on the feast-days of the Chöjong, the 9th, 19th, and 29th of the moon, lamas are ready to attend, bringing on these occasions their trumpets as well as drums and cymbals, and making a great noise all day long.

But the most notable observances of the whole twelve months are those held at the New Year. During the seven days from the 23rd to the 29th of the 12th moon the lamas are in the house, where large, vase-shaped dorma have been set up ; and the thump of drums, the clash of cymbals, and the drone of trumpets never cease. On the 29th the dorma are burned in a little straw hut put up just outside the house ; and so all the evil and all the bad luck of the past year are consumed, and the new year starts fair.

The second act falls on the third day of the new year, when the lamas come to the house and make fresh chöba for the chöjong in the chapel. The family treasure-chest, "yanggam," is then opened ; its contents are laid as an offering beside the chöba and blessed, and thus left out for a period of from three to seven days.

Finally, on the day when the treasure-chest is to be closed, the lamas reappear, and a draba is sent up to the roof, carrying a plate of tsamba in his left hand and an arrow, bound with silk streamers of five different colours, in his right. Waving the arrow he calls : "Come, luck ! Come, luck ! " The arrow is called "dadar." It is decorated with turquoise and coral, and attached to it is a metal mirror, "melong." Its five silk ribbons are "lucky signs," the stones are "precious signs," and the mirror attracts luck. The dadar figures also at baptisms, marriages, seed-sowing, and like occasions.

The chest is now sealed up and the lamas and members of the family all help themselves to a pinch of tsamba from the draba's plate. Then, gathering round a large basin or bag filled with dry tsamba, which stands in the middle of the room, they take out handfuls and throw them at each other, shouting: "Come, luck! Come, luck!" Soon everyone is covered with meal and the floor of the room is white. As red is the auspicious colour in China, so is white in Tibet, and the throwing of the tsamba signifies "A Happy New Year!"—a wish that, in the year just begun, the house and its inmates will always be white, that is, have the best of luck. This ceremony is known as "Yangdrub," the "gathering of luck," and with modifications to suit varying degrees of fortune it is celebrated in every home in Tibet.

An occasion which provides the Tibetans with an opportunity of indulging both their taste for religious ceremonial and their love of "picnicking" is the worship of the mountain spirits, or "Yül-lha"—country gods. On every mountain in Tibet lives a spirit who is either good or bad. They have lived there from time immemorial and no one knows their origin any more than he knows whence came Drasrinmo, who, however, unlike them, possessed a physical body. The bad spirit is called Zhidag; if regularly worshipped, he will be beneficent; if neglected, he will send snowstorms to ruin the fields and destroy the yak. He must be visited and worshipped at a stated time each year, which is in the 4th, 5th, or 6th moon, varying with the locality. On these occasions great numbers flock out to the Zhidag's mountain, taking their families with them and tents in which to camp for a day or two of holiday. To the spirit they offer tea, wine, milk, and barley, (but never flesh), erect prayer-flags and burn juniper. This duty over, they devote the rest of the outing to having a good time; and with horse-racing, archery, foot-races, dancing, singing, and drinking, all are jolly. The lamas, too, find diversion in a picnic, and frequently camp out for several days, the older ones enjoying the alfresco tea-drinking and the extra relish of food, telling stories, and discussing points of doctrine, while the younger run races, dance, sing, drink, gamble and "talk nonsense."

On the other hand the good spirit, Ne or Neri, is always kind, whether you make him offerings or not. He sends you good crops and assures you of Dewajen when you die. Worship of the Ne takes the form of circumambulating the mountain on which he lives, such pilgrimages being made either singly or in parties, and at any time convenient to the pilgrim.

To Lhasa all Tibetans, irrespective of sex and religious sect, make at least one pilgrimage in the course of their lives, for no Tibetan dies easy in mind if he has not seen the Jowo in the Jokang, and thus been purified of sin. As a rule, owing to the number of robbers on the roads, no money is taken on this journey; only blankets to sleep in and felts to afford protection from the rain and snow. Pilgrims carry money only if accompanying a caravan large enough to ensure immunity from attack, in which case they do the journey in comfort. In the matter of food their tastes are simple, and they can always depend for tea and tsamba on the hospitality of the people through whose country they pass. From Kam to Lhasa the journey takes four or five months, the northern or trade route being avoided because of the food difficulty. If, as is usually the case, they diverge from the track to visit other holy places in the neighbourhood, it may easily take them six.*

A certain kind of ascetic, known as "jangchaba," measures the whole distance on his stomach ; that is to say, he lies flat and knocks his head on the ground, rises and walks the length of his body, lies down again, and so on. Such pilgrims take four or five years to accomplish the journey, and are held in high esteem ever afterwards. Some of them, it is true, abandon this form of progression when they believe no eye to be upon them ; on the other hand many have such keen consciences that they will not cross a river by boat without measuring its breadth by rope and putting in the extra distance on shore.

Lamas who feel guilty of sin make pilgrimage to the chief lamaseries of their respective sects. The Geluba go to Lhasa, where are the Drebung, Serra, and Galden monasteries, and some few to Drashilhunbo ; the Karjuba go to Dölung Tsurbu, or to Barbung in Derge ; the Sachyaba to Sachya Kung or the neighbouring Ngor ; and the Nyimaba to Dsogchen, Gartog, or Beyü, in Derge, for the Mindroling and the Dorjedrag at Lhasa are not very special. The priests of the Bönbo go to Mensre, ten days beyond Lhasa, as well as to Lhasa itself.

* For road taken by pilgrims, see Itinerary in Appendix No. 2.

CHAPTER V

BIRTH, INFANCY, AND ADOLESCENCE.

A child without parentage—Beliefs regarding childbirth—Baptismal ceremony—Loss of memory—Schooling—Dice and Beer—The Lamaist novice.

THE new-born Tibetan babe is not the child of its parents, at least in the sense understood in western countries. True, it gets its body from them, the father supplying the bones and the mother the flesh, but the individual life is an entire stranger. You must remember its history. After leaving purgatory, where the Judge has doomed it to re-birth in "Man's Country," and searching anxiously for a favourable haven, it finds what it wants, if it is very knowledgeful, or takes the first chance that offers if it is not, and so enters again on the Wheel of Life.

The Tibetan woman is fortunate above others in accomplishing her childbirth easily. She may go to the mountain for wood and bring back a child in her gown. But she does not like anyone to know the time when she is to give birth. For if a single person knows, the birth will be delayed for an hour; if two persons know, it is delayed for two hours; if many know, the delivery will be very difficult, being delayed perhaps five, six, or seven days.

There is no period of seclusion, and ordinarily the mother is at work again next day. In Tibetan houses the ground floor is a stable for yak, sheep, and other animals; the family lives in the first storey ; the flat roof is used in praying to the good and evil spirits. It is bad to be delivered on the roof, in the open air ; childbirth is easiest close to earth, so the expectant mother goes to the stable, which has no wooden floor and which, besides, is the most private part of the house ; also there may be an idea that delivery among the cattle will be as easy as that of the cattle themselves. There is no doctor of course ; if the woman is rich, she will take a servant with her ; if poor, she goes alone.

The babe is born on a rug or felt, richer persons using a hair mattress. It is not washed, merely wiped, and a little butter is put on the fontanel, in the belief that it will strengthen that part of the cranium. For the first three days it is wrapped not in new clothes but in the old undergarments of its parents, which are soft, and have implicit in them the warm affection of father and mother. The afterbirth, which is thrown away, is called colloquially in Dartsendo "Birth Friend" (Jyerog).

On the third day the lama is brought in to "give power" (tse-wang, life-power) and baptise the child. As already noted, the child bears no relation to its parents, so surnames do not exist. The personal name is chosen not by the parents but by the lama, and always consists of four syllables, the first two of which, in 50 per cent. of cases, indicate the particular sect to which the lama belongs, and are known as the "religious name." Thus :—

Pedma is the favourite in the Nyima sect.
Lozang or Jamba ,, ,, Gelug sect.
Karma ,, ,, Karju sect.
Gunka ,, ,, Sachya sect, while
Yungdrung is favoured by the Bönbo.

Girls' names are different from boys, and are retained by them after marriage. In Kam, if the mother has had more than one child that died, she will ask the lama not to give the new baby a "religious name" but a "Yama name," Yama being goddesses who protect children. Names may afterwards be changed ; for example, in cases of severe sickness the lama may decide that the misfortune is due to a wrong name having been given, and the patient must be rebaptised. In rare instances the lama is not called in at all, and the child retains its pet name through life—"Patru" ("piggy") or "Chitru" ("doggy"), as the case may be. An old man in the service of the Mission next door is still called "Patru"; he has never "received power," and is rather stupid. Poor people sometimes wait for one year before calling the lama, although the fee is only two or three rupees, or a brick or two of tea. Among nomads baptism is frequently late ; a nomad chief, whom I shall tell of by and by, was as a baby called "Wednesday," because he was born on that day, and, in spite of the fact that he was afterwards "given power," the name Headman Wednesday still clings to him.

On his arrival, the lama proceeds to arrange the chöba on a table at the end of the room. The "life-power chöba" takes the following form :—

1. Seven bowls of brass or silver, two of which contain water, and the other five respectively (a) a mirror, representing "sight"; (b) cymbals, "hearing"; (c) incense, "smell"; (d) tsamba and rice, "taste"; (e) silk or cloth, "feeling."

2. In the middle, behind this row, is the Vase of Life (tse-bum) empty, standing on a plate. Alongside of it is a plate containing Pills of Life (tse-ril),

little balls of tsamba mixed with butter and sugar. On the other side of it is a skull-cup containing beer sweetened with sugar (tse-chang), and a baptismal pot (bumba) clothed in a petticoat of the five lucky colours, and holding some peacock feathers or sacred kusha grass. The bumba contains saffron water.

3. Behind this second row are seven dorma, of the bottle-shaped variety already described; and against the wall, point downward, is the Arrow of Life (tse-dar) with its five coloured streamers.

Sitting alongside the table, with a draba in attendance, the lama calls for the father or mother, or both, to fetch the child. They bring it in, its old clothes being discarded in favour of new ones, and sit in front of the chöba. The lama gives them a little water to rinse the mouth, and then from the bumba pours some saffron water on the heads of each of the three; or, he uses the peacock feathers or the kusha grass to sprinkle them. With a bell in his left hand and a damaru (skull-drum) on a table near his right, he then reads the scriptures for a long time, ringing the bell and rattling the drum to invoke the God of Life (Tse-lha or Tsebame—Amitayus or Aparamitayus). When the god has entered the Vase, the lama raises the plate with the Vase on it and places it on the heads of father, mother, and child, saying "Tsebame is in this Vase." Then he takes the Arrow of Life and waves it four times in the direction of the four points of the compass, so that more life may come into the child. From the skull-cup he takes a spoonful of tse-chang and puts some in the hands of the father and mother, who drink of it and put a little in the child's mouth; and he gives each parent three tse-ril, which they eat, putting a portion of them in the child's mouth. Then he lays his dorje on the child's back, shoulders, and head, saying: "This dorje will make a tent of protection about you."* And he takes a kada of coloured silk and, knotting it in the middle to represent a dorje, places it round the child's neck, saying: "This child is called so-and-so; may he be lucky!"

The ceremony, which has lasted half a day, or even the whole day, is now over. It is the same for boys and for girls and is called "Tse-wang Gug," "invoking life-power." Tea and tsamba are served to the lama, the fee is paid, and he departs.

"Mother" in Tibetan is "Ma," or "Ama"; "father" is "Pa"; a wet-nurse is "Ma-ma." If poor persons require a wet-nurse, they get a relative for the office; the rich employ a stranger who is clean and strong; very poor people, obliged to go out to work, leave the baby on the mattress, tied by a string to keep it out of danger. Father, mother, and relative like to take turns in nursing the baby in the breast of their gowns. The baby does not have diapers of course, and naturally accidents happen in the breast pocket, but nobody minds trifles like that.

Man's sorrows begin in his mother's womb. He is scalded by a hot drink and frozen by a cold; pain pursues him in his egress from the womb and his fall on the floor.

The child's memory of a former existence, and of the judgment of the King of Hell, fresh when he is newly born, gradually becomes dimmer with each new lesson learnt, until it finally disappears. When

* Among northern Buddhists the dorje is the ritual sceptre of the priests, a symbol of power, which they hold while they pray, moving it about in various directions.—*Jaes.*, p. 287.

only a few days old, he attains sufficient strength to hold his head erect, and in the achievement forgets a little. After five months he begins to recognise his father's and mother's faces and, as he laughs, forgets a little. In six months he has learned to use his hands to pull things or shake things, and he can sit up; he forgets more. At eight months he begins to use his teeth, and forgets more. At nine months he is crawling on all fours and continues to forget. At twelve months he learns to stand upright and walk, forgetting more, and every time he falls he loses memories. When he learns to talk, all his memories vanish.

At seven or eight years the boy begins to learn his A, B, C—in Tibetan, Gaka (written "Ka-k'a'), these being the first two letters of the alphabet—and afterwards is taught short prayers and stories from the Legshe, a book of fables compiled by a Sachya lama. There are no regular schools; but there is usually a scholar in the village who teaches boys in his own house. Rich people employ a tutor at home for their children, instead of sending them to the village teacher. Writing, which is considered important, takes several years to learn. Poor boys start earning their tsamba at eight years of age by looking after yak, sheep, horses, etc., and at 15 or 16 are doing a man's work and thinking of marriage. Before settling down in life, they usually make the pilgrimage to Lhasa: a girl who has not been there is looked at askance by match-making parents; her chances are distinctly less bright.* There are no games, but men play dice and drink chang at the

* "In the Mi-nyag district (west of Tachienlu) it is very rare for unmarried girls to visit Lhasa. I know of only one case."—J. H. E.

inns. Tibetans are lazy and very fond of chang; they do not take life very seriously.

If a family has two sons, one of them at least, more especially if he happens to be physically weak, is destined for the priesthood, the belief being that, by entering the church he will get well and live long.* So, when three or four years of age—the earlier the better—he is taken to a lamasery, where he will be given a "religious name" if his own is not of that character. The ceremony is similar to, but less elaborate than, the baptism at three days, and is known as "sermingdag." On its completion he is given a red, yellow, or orange gown to wear, but without committing him to the sect which favours the particular colour; such commitment comes later and is ordinarily decided by the boy's father. The parents present the lama with the usual kada and some trankas or rupees and bring the boy home again. The Bönbo have a similar ceremony.

When from 8 to 10 years of age the boy is sent to live at the lamasery, the parents presenting it with a boilerful of tea and choosing a gegen from among the lamas. The pupil lives with his gegen and spends most of his day reading aloud and memorising the scriptures, which the gegen hears him repeat by heart in the evening. But as he acquires them parrot-fashion, without understanding the meaning, he never learns to think. This is one of the obstacles which the foreign missionary encounters; persons to whom tracts are distributed may be able to read them, but never having been taught to think, have

* Waddell puts the proportion of priests in Tibet at one out of every six or eight of the population.

not the wit to understand unless the text is carefully explained.

While living at the lamasery, the pupil is allowed to receive occasional presents of food from home. After a few years, but not before he has reached the age of 16, when he has learned to read well, he goes through the ceremony of "drapulenba." A barber cuts his hair, all except one lock, which is then severed by the abbot (kanbo), who gives him another name, and he becomes a Genyen, or clerical apprentice, the first ot the two stages of the noviciate. When he is 20 years of age he may become a Getsul, or under-priest, the second stage of the noviciate; and at any time during this noviciate he may try an examination for a B.D. degree and, if he passes, is called Geshi. But he is still a *draba;* the fully ordained priest is called a Gelong.* The several sects differ greatly in the attention they give to study: the Nyima lamas are generally well-trained students, and keep up their religious studies, whereas many Geluba cannot even read, but just wear the dress and live in the monastery. Perhaps it is for this reason that the latter are more conservative.

* "The Buddhism of Tibet is usually called Lamaism, the word 'lama,' meaning 'the superior one,' being that given by Chinese and foreigners generally to the members of the Buddhist monastic order in Tibet. In Tibet, however, this word is reserved for those monks who have not only taken the highest theological degrees, but who have also led a saintly life and become famed for their knowledge. The word *draba* is used by Tibetans as a general term for all persons connected with the order, monks as well as lay brethren."—*Rock.*, Notes, p. 730.

It would appear that fully-ordained priesthood does not require a Geshi degree, and that the ordinary Gelong does not command such veneration as a Geshi.

CHAPTER VI

ON MARRIAGE CUSTOMS.

Early Marriage—Horoscopes—" Begging Beer "—The Armed Horsemen—The Orator—" Breast Money "—The Bride brought Home—Rice-throwing—A Dowry on Paper—The Wedding Feast—Irregular Marriage—Marriage by Capture—Divorce—Polygamy—Polyandry.

WHEN a boy is from 16 to 20 years of age, his parents begin to look out for a wife for him. This is four or five years earlier than was the custom in the last generation, but people marry younger nowadays because we are approaching the Tselojuba period.

Having fixed on a girl a year or two younger than his son, and otherwise suitable, the father first of all makes private enquiries among friends with a view to ascertaining the character of her horoscope. This information he communicates to a soothsayer (tsi-ba), who compares it with the boy's horoscope. Time is counted in cycles of sixty years, and each year is called by a name combining one of the five elements—earth, fire, water, wood, iron—with one of twelve different animals, so that we have earth-horse year, fire-horse year, etc. If the tsiba finds that the combinations in the respective birth-years harmonise, all will be well. For example, the horse and sheep, being "very friendly," make the best union ; wood, earth, and fire are all very friendly ; water and fire naturally do not go well together ; and the pig, which signifies laziness and stupidity, does not match happily with the serpent, which is emblematic of anger.

Suppose it is my boy that is getting married. If the two horoscopes are harmonious, I then get the tsiba to choose a middle-man to approach the girl's father. The latter gives the middle-man tsamba, meat, tea, beer, etc. ; and after eating and drinking, the subject of the proposed marriage is introduced. The girl's father and mother say that they will think about it and give an answer after three days, or after seven days. When that time has elapsed, they give their answer to the middle-man, and if it is favourable, I send them a present of meat and beer with a kada. This present is known as "long chang," "begging beer," that is, beer sent when begging for the girl, and acceptance of it by the father and mother implies promise of their daughter's hand.

The middle-man returns and informs me that the begging beer has been accepted, and enquires when the wedding is to take place. I reply, in so many weeks or months or years. When the time draws near, I call the tsiba again, who selects an auspicious day. I then kill sheep and yak, and brew beer, and get new clothes and boots for my boy and the girl, also ornaments from the silversmith ; and the girl's parents do the same.

The day before the wedding I send horsemen to the girl's house, armed with bows, swords, guns, and spears, and carrying charms (ga-u). At intervals on the road they stop to rest and sit cross-legged on the ground, singing and playing and drinking beer, very happy. On their arrival, the parents come out of the house with plates of tsamba and butter, and wave the luck-arrow (dadar), with its silk streamers of red, yellow, white, blue, and green, and cry "Welcome!" Waving the arrow three times means: "May you bring luck with you!" The horsemen then partake of the tsamba and butter, but only a very little, to show that they are men of substance, no "empty mouths" among them, and go into the house.

Inside they sit down in order on long rugs, the big man at the far end of the room and the man of least consequence nearest to the door. Seniority is determined first by official rank, then by reputation as an orator, then by wealth, and finally by age. They drink tea and beer and milk, and eat tsamba and meat and everything good. After the feast they sing and dance and play and do not go to bed that night. The man who is most clever with words makes an address or prayer to all the gods, in which he says: "In the sky are the sun and the moon and the eight great stars—all beautiful; may the house of this boy and girl be equally beautiful, bright, and glorious! The earth is full of flowers and trees and men and animals; may this house also be fruitful! The Nag country is jewelful and has eight rich kings; may this house have all the luck that precious jewels bring!"

While these festivities are going on, the girl remains all the time in her room and is not seen. After the feast I send the "nu-ring," milk-money (literally "breast-money"), to the father and mother in recognition of their having brought up the girl. It is not a big present, only some silver, or tea, or a horse.

Next day, at an hour given by the tsiba, the girl is brought out and handed over to the horsemen;

some women accompany her. Anything from five to fifty horsemen form up in front, with the same number behind, and the girl with the women in the middle. The leading horseman carries a picture to frighten off evil spirits, which is called Jungwa Kuntub or Sepachagja ("please all make way!"). As they ride off, the girl's parents at the house-door wave the dadar and call loudly "Yang kor lo!" (come back, luck!) and the horsemen shout back "Yang nga tso dang nyamburshö" (come with us, luck!). It is just as if they were fighting: "You say you want with you; I say I want with me!" but nobody is angry, it is only make-believe.

When they arrive at my house, they find the tsiba at the door with books for exorcising devils, and plenty of wheat, rice, barley, and small black and white pebbles, all mixed up. Before letting the girl enter the house, he reads from the books, praying that the grain and stones will have power like bullets to drive away the devils. The girl stands with her face covered by a cloth, white, yellow, or red in colour. The tsiba throws the grain and small stones on the girl, thereby driving away any devil or ghost or bad spirit that may be with her, and she is then brought into the house. The crossing of the threshold may be said to constitute the marriage formality; there is no other.

The girl's parents send with her a long list of presents—yak, horses, sheep, wheat, jewellery, cloth, gold, silver—but not the presents themselves. By and by, perhaps after seven or eight years, if my boy still loves that girl, and if that girl still loves my boy, and both are very happy, her parents will send the presents written on the list.

Feasting then begins. All the horsemen and friends and relatives eat and drink and speak nonsense and talk very happy. Some get drunk. The two mothers are busy cooking the food and, if the girl's father is old, he may not come but will sit at home twirling a prayer-wheel and repeating "Om-Mani-Pedme-Hum!" Those who are not drunk start dancing and singing again, women dancing with women, and men with men, and for several days a lama sits in a corner reading from two books, the "Drashidsikba" and the "Namsa Nangje." The lama's readings are a mediation between the young couple and the Universe of Earth, Sky, and Nag. Sometimes the boy and girl go to the roof with their friends, wave the dadar, burn juniper in the stove there, and beg the gods to help them.

The feasting lasts for one or two weeks or months, no certain time; but after the first day or two, the tsiba names an auspicious day for the girl to sleep in my boy's room. The old women prepare the room and occupy it until dusk, when they bring the girl to it and leave her there. My boy and the horsemen take no notice, all dancing and singing. By and by, in order to deceive the boy, about 10 or 11 o'clock, the guests pretend to be sleepy and want to retire, so the boy goes to his room. After that, the guests may, if they are really tired, go to bed or they may stay up and sing and dance and tell stories; but nobody takes any notice of the boy and the girl.

In many cases among the poorer people there is no formal marriage like this. Occasionally a young couple without parents, or too poor to afford the expense of a proper marriage, bind themselves by solemn declaration to be true to each other and never to marry anyone else, and they tell their friends that they have done so. This is considered sufficient, even without witnesses, though in popular opinion the presence of witnesses make the ceremony more regular. They set up house together or, as it is called, "light a fire," and are regarded as husband and wife. This custom is the usual one among the lower classes in Dartsendo.

If a boy and girl are sweethearts (ning-dug) they exchange boot-garters in token of the fact ; but this does not signify engagement to marry. Sometimes, as when they have to part for a short time, there may be an exchange of rings, but merely as souvenirs. If there is a child, they generally marry, but there is no social obligation on them to do so ; they please themselves. Tibetans are not hard on a girl who has a child by an unknown father. If her parents can persuade her to divulge the man's name, they will make a fuss ; if they cannot, they make the best of it. She is regarded as not very good, but is not harshly condemned ; and never in any case, even during quarrels and abuse, is the child taunted as a bastard. In Lhasa they do not have the custom of exchanging garters and rings.

Very often among the nomads of northern Tibet a girl is robbed away ; and the same happens sometimes in Kanze and Litang districts. A young Golok courting a girl goes to see her every evening, and one night may stay till morning. If the father objects, the suitor gets his friends together and, armed with guns, swords, and spears, they ride over to the tent and carry off the girl. Sometimes they carry off yak and horses as well. The father pursues the bridegroom and, if he can, will kill him and bring the girl back. The brother or nephew of the dead man then takes up the feud, seeking revenge. The girl so captured may be from the nomad's own tribe, or from a different one, according to his personal fancy. Sometimes it is a married woman who is robbed away, and in this case, if caught, her nose and hair are cut off and she is sent away.

Divorce is a simple matter. If, after marriage, that girl turns out to be lazy and unkind, or if she proves barren, she can be sent back to her father, but the boy must pay her father in horses, yak, tea, or cloth. The affair starts by the boy speaking hard words to his wife, beating her, and pushing her out. She complains to her father, who sends for a middle-man to arrange the matter. The middle-man is a friend and does not get paid for his services, only receives meals while negotiating. Having talked to the boy and found that he is quite determined on divorce, he reports this to the father, and suggests that the two people are not a happy match and that there will only be more trouble if they live together. The matter then becomes one of bargaining. The boy offers one horse, the father demands ten. Eventually the middle-man decides that three horses, or four, are adequate compensation in the circumstances, and his decision is final: he refuses to talk any more on the subject, and father and husband acquiesce in it. If there are children of the marriage, the father invariably keeps the sons, but sometimes a daughter may go back with the mother.

If a man's sister-in-law is attractive and comes to work for him, it is not unusual for her to share the nuptial couch, in which case the man is regarded as having two wives. After keeping her for two or three years, he establishes a claim on her as a wife, which is recognised, more especially if there are children. Also, if a man has no sons, but only daughters, he adopts a son and gives him his eldest daughter in marriage. When the second daughter grows up, she too may be given to him, but without form of marriage. Although rare in Lhasa, this custom is quite common in Kam in the case of two sisters, and instances of three are known.

Alongside this form of polygamy with sisters exists polyandry with brothers. It also is quite common in Kam. Among the nomads, however, polyandry does not occur and polygamy very rarely.* As the sexes are about equal in number, polyandry cannot be due to the scarcity of women, of whom about half remain unmarried (though not usually childless), and many, in recent years at least, have gone off with Chinese soldiers. In fact, the balance is the other way ; owing to the number of men who enter the Church, there are more women than men available for marriage. Polyandry is found only in farming districts and is due to the family's fear of poverty. If three brothers were to marry three separate wives and set up three separate establishments, the field inherited from their father would have to be divided up. They therefore share a wife ; and the children, whoever the actual begetter may be, are held to belong to the eldest brother, the others being regarded as uncles. Of the three brothers, one will look after the farm, another travel on business, or perhaps join the nomads, and the

* J. H. E. informs me that the nomads around Litang seem peculiarly around to polyandry.

one who is a lama, when he returns home on a visit, will also claim conjugal rights.* I am told that at Kanze they have a custom that, when one of her husbands visits the wife in her private room at night, he hangs his rosary on her door; should another husband come in, he will feel for the rosary, and if it is there, will quietly retire. Polygamy and polyandry are known as Zasumba. I might mention that a custom which is common enough is for a man to allow a close personal friend to share his wife's favours; I have known such cases in Dartsendo, Kanze, Gyangtse, Darjeeling, and elsewhere.†

When I stayed at Dawu, my landlord had three sons. The eldest was educated in the local lamasery and afterwards sent to Lhasa. On his return he saw a girl in the Dawu valley whom he liked very much. As she also loved him, he took her away. The two fathers sent horsemen after the pair, caught them, and brought them back to Dawu, but did not punish either. But neither of the fathers gave any presents to the couple, the one because he had spent much on his son's education, the other because his daughter had disregarded his advice and had further sinned in giving her affections to a lama. These two are still living in Dawu, but their fathers will have nothing to do with them.

The second brother married in accordance with

* "The 'Hsi Tsang T'u K'ao' mentions that polyandry is of great value in certain circumstances in the interests of union; that is, the woman is a centre round which certain satellites revolve."—J. H. E.

† Père Goré states: "On rencontre encore des cas curieux, celui de deux amis dont les intérêts sont communs et qui ne prennent qu'une seule femme, ou bien celui d'un tiers entrant comme nouveau mari dans un ménage deja constitué. Ces sortes d'unions n'existent qu'autant que les intérêts sont communs, et souvent le mari trop complaisant se voit chassé et par son associé et par sa femme."

his father's wishes, had two daughters, and then died. By this time the third brother had reached the age of about 20 and, with the approval of his father, took over his brother's wife. He adopted this course because, if she were sent back to her father, it would mean incurring a large expenditure; he would have done just the same thing if one of his deceased brother's children had been a son. Had he married another woman, he would have had to incur the expense of either returning the widow to her father or keeping her, an extra mouth, in his own house.* In cases like this no form of marriage is gone through: the widow simply goes to the man. She may not be what he himself would have chosen, but morals all over Tibet are quite easy in these matters, and he could at any time suit his own taste outside.

* That is, the reason was economic: it was not a case of "raising up seed" to his deceased brother.

CHAPTER VII

SICKNESS, DEATH, AND THE HEREAFTER.

Moba and Moma—Sickness caused by Tutelaries—By the Nag—By Dre—The Podeb Lama—49 Days' Wandering—The Bardo Trong—Before the King of Hell—Dewajen—Man's Country—Yidag—Lha—Hinayana and Mahayana—The Story of Jungdsega's Conversion.

WHEN a man is sick, or angry without knowing why, he sends for the soothsayer, known as the Mo-ba, or goes to him with a kada and some money, and begs him to tell him what is wrong. In the same way a woman consults the Mo-ma. Every Tibetan is more or less able to tell fortunes by rosaries, dice, etc., but, while the lamas of course are professionals,* the Moba and Moma also command respect as adepts. The Moba will tell the sick man that a certain Chöjong, or Lhamo, or the Nag, or a Dre, is angry with him.

Everyone in Tibet believes in these powerful agencies; and every house has a little room called the Chökang in which is a picture of the particular Chöjong or Lhamo in whom he trusts for protection. So, if the Moba tells you which Chöjong or Lhamo is angry, you go to the lamasery, call a lama, tell him your trouble, and ask him to read your Chöjong's or Lhamo's Gangso. These are books of ritual for placating the tutelaries, each tutelary having one proper to itself. If the patient is well-to-do, with

* In Tachienlu a lama, known by the Chinese name Sung, enjoys a wide reputation for accuracy in fortune-telling, and is consulted regularly by Chinese officials, from the Commissioner downwards.

servants who can attend on the lamas, the latter are sent for, and the service is held in the sick person's chökang; otherwise he sends money to the lamasery with a request that prayers be offered for him. In one of the rooms of the lamasery are pictures and images of the chöjong and lhamo, and the lama goes to the one favoured by the sick man and reads from his gangso for one or two days. At the end of the reading he will tell you that he has interceded for you to the best of his power, and he hopes that you will now be better, but he cannot assure you definitely that his prayers will be heard.

If it is the Nag that is angry, you generally know without consulting the Moba, because it is he who sends boils, sore eyes, rheumatism, leprosy, etc., to those who pollute water. Then the sick man must get the lama to make peace with the Nag. In this case the lama does not read a gangso, but goes to a spring in the hills, taking with him new wool of all colours—red, yellow, black, white, blue, etc.; also some white goat's milk; red cow's milk; butter, flour, and sugar; also gold, silver, copper, iron, turquoise, and coral; branches of pine and juniper; and prayer flags. All these things are supplied by the sick man, the metals being merely sample grains. The place visited must be a spring, the river will not do, because the spring comes direct from the Nag. The branches and prayer flags are planted round the spring, the wool is stuck on the branches, and the offerings are thrown into the water. The lama then reads the Nag prayer-book for two or three hours. The same ceremony is observed when praying the Nag to send rain. The lama's fee is generally a rupee, less in the case of poor people, from whom he is content to receive a little tea or barley.

In certain circumstances the spirit of a dead man (namshe) does not go to the King of Hell but remains behind, haunting the place where the man died. This angry ghost is then known as a Dre. It may be said that there are four sets of circumstances which produce Dre. First is the case of men who have been killed by the sword or other weapon. Second is that of the rich man of material mind who is indifferent to the promptings of his soul and who, even on his death bed, does not think of where his soul may be going, but only of all the possessions he is leaving behind. Third may be classed those who die suddenly of a seizure; these are believed to have been killed by a spirit. And fourth come those who have died a violent death by accident or suicide. The Dre of the fourth class are known as Rock Spirits, Water Spirits, Fire Spirits, and Wood Spirits. The ghost of a man killed by falling from a rock lives in the rock and tries to kill other men in the same way. The ghost of a man who is drowned lives in the water and tries to drag in anyone walking near-by. The ghost of a man who has been burned to death haunts the place and causes fires. And the ghost of a man who has hanged himself on a tree lives in the tree and tries to induce others to follow his example.

If the Moba decides that the sick man's trouble is caused by a Dre, he will tell him that certain books must be read and offerings made (dü or lü). The offerings consist of images in tsamba of a man, representing the patient, and sometimes also of his wife and family and his cattle, horses, yak, and sheep; similar images in wood of guns, swords, and arrows; threads of all colours; silk, cloth, silver, rice, barley. All these are arranged as a chöba in the chökang and many lamas come. The head lama sits nearest to the chöba, and the rest, in parallel rows, down to the door. In addition to the bell, which all the lamas carry, the head lama has a small damaru, two others have Po (Ch., cymbals), two have small trumpets, two have medium-sized trumpets about two feet long, two have trumpets of ten to fifteen feet, two have conch-shells, and half a dozen have big drums. For seven days and nights continuously the lamas read and "beat the drum." They have regular days for starting the performance, namely the "good luck days" on which the Lhasang is held, and they thus end on the chöjong feast days, the 9th, 19th, and 29th of the moon. On the seventh day the dü is taken out of the house, placed in straw, and burned, the orchestra making a great noise all the time. The head lama informs the Dre responsible for the sickness that he herewith hands over to him the offending person, his wife and family, and all his possessions; in return for which the Dre must not come near the house again. The lamas are then paid off and go home, the fee being one rupee per day each, the head lama receiving two rupees.

Next morning the Moba is again consulted and, after various forms of divination, advises the patient: "Your mo-mo is more promising, but you had better offer another dü, a small one will be enough, and get two lamas to read." The same performance, but on a much modified scale, is then repeated; perhaps only half a catty of tsamba is used and the ceremony lasts only half a day. On the same evening, before sunset, the dü is taken out of the house and deposited at a bridgehead and at cross-roads, so as to intercept the Dre whichever way he may come.

If even this does not produce the desired effect, and the man continues sick, the Moba will come to the conclusion that the Dre must be inside him, and must be exorcised by a Jöba lama. The latter, therefore, comes to the patient's house after dark with a big damaru, a bell, and a thigh-bone trumpet. All the lights in the room are extinguished and the Jöba puts a black bearskin on his head. He blows his trumpet three times, rings the bell, rattles the damaru, and recites incantations to call the Dre to him. When the Dre comes he talks kindly to it, expostulating with it for visiting this poor ignorant man, and offering himself as a ransom in his place. While talking to the Dre he keeps ringing the bell and rattling the drum ; and this may last for an hour. Eventually the lama leaves, telling the sick man that he hopes he will now be well, but making no promise.

This procedure obtains all over Tibet. Although the people have no great faith in its efficacy, they are obliged by general opinion to keep it up. For, if a man's father were to die without the Moba being consulted, and every possible chance of saving him tried, the relatives would have uneasy consciences for the rest of their lives.

All Dre are malicious, but they can be placated. For instance, if I know of a tree on which a man has hanged himself, I go there and burn juniper to him and hang up pieces of cloth and offer him tea and tsamba. Then he will not harm me. But generally you do not know, and then you must depend on the lamas, for they are the only persons who can actually see the Dre. When a Dre becomes too wicked and kills people, a lama goes to the haunted place and reads incantations, perhaps also erects a chöden or a mani, in order to drive it away. If the Dre is powerful and refuses to be driven out, the lama tries another plan and, speaking kindly to it, offers to provide it with a proper abode and to procure worship for it. The place he gives it will be a rock or a tree or a little stone house (lha-to or lha-dsug), like that you see on the mountain side near Dorje Drag, plastered and coloured red, measuring perhaps five feet by six. And the Dre will be worshipped as a Dsen or a Jelbo or such small deity. Other Dre are deified as Lhamo, etc., and their lhato may be coloured red, or yellow, or white, but red is always the colour for Dsen and Jelbo even in the Geluba sect. People go there and offer tea, beer, and tsamba, hang up prayer flags, kadas, and pieces of cloth of the five colours—red, yellow, green, blue, and white—and burn juniper and incense. If the Dsen or the Jelbo does good work, approved by the lamas who are watching its behaviour, it will be rewarded by being made a Chöjong or guardian of the faith. A special gangso will be written for it ; its picture will be painted and hung in the Chöjong room of the lamasery ; and in due course the Chöjong may attain to Jangchub Jisa, the highest stage of Bodhisatship and next to Nirvana.

In the monastery of Samye, the oldest in Tibet, are two of these deified Dre, a Dsen and a Jelbo. The Dsen is the spirit of a man that died in battle.

As a deity he is known as Dsimara, one of the Chöjong of the Geluba, and is always consulted before battle. There is a big ceremony with "beating the drum," and a lama or other person enters, dressed as Dsimara. Questions are put to the Dsen, who enters the body of his impersonator and replies through him. The impersonator is a Chöje (Lord of the Faith) or Gutenba. The Jelbo in Samye is the spirit of a very wise lama, full of knowledge of the scriptures, called Shugden, who in some way when alive displeased the Lhasa Government and was thrown into the river. His Dre in due course became a Jelbo ; and now the Geluba and Satchyaba revere and worship him as one of the greatest of their Chöjong.

Of course it sometimes happens that the Dre refuses to be placated even by the offer of a permanent abode and worship, and he continues to kill people. In this case the lamas dig a hole in which they bury the Dre and erect a black chöden above it. Sometimes the chöden is placed upside down. Although the Dre is still alive, he cannot get out ; and people passing by may hear him uttering imprecations. The Nyagdrül Chöden at Lhasa is a black one, erected over a Chantui Hutuktu who was put in prison in Lhasa and committed suicide by cutting his throat.

Dre less powerful than these, unable to do much serious mischief, are hunted about from place to place. There are very many of them in the world. They have a meeting-place at a lamasery in Nepal, which Pedma Rinchen and I visited. In the temple of the lamasery, where they assemble after dark, is a spring, burning all the time with a blue flame.

If, in spite of all that the lamas can do, the sick man dies, then a high lama is sent for, who is called the Podeb Lama because he opens the way to heaven ; in Chinese he is "k'ai lu lama." The Podeb lama is like a strong archer, he can send the soul straight as an arrow to Dewajen. The ordinary lama cannot help the spirit to escape from judgment by the King of Hell, and subsequent despatch to one or other of the six Gati, but he believes that the Podeb may have this power. On the third day, when the spirit awakes, it is much more clever than during life and, if the family conceives any doubts about the ability of the Podeb, on that day a "Third-day Podeb" (zhagsum Podeb) is sent for. A Dsalung lama is the most powerful kind of Podeb ; he is a wizard.

First the Podeb pulls the hair of the dead man. If he is not actually dead, but only unconscious and now opens his eyes, it is very good, because he can then understand a little. If he is really dead, the spirit may be hiding in the room under something heavy. Then the lama will say, "Heek! Pett!" nine times and the spirit will jump up, raising the heavy article with it. The lama makes the spirit go back into the body, not through any of the nine orifices, but through the dsa-wuma or blood-vessels.* He tells it that, being now dead, it is no use to think more about this world ; it must think instead about the next. In the Bardo are about one hundred roads of different colours, but he must choose the white one ; for it alone leads to Dewajen, the abode of Amitabha or Obame. He describes the dangers

* According to Tibetan theory there are three principal veins proceeding from the heart : Wuma, the middle one, is white ; Changma, the left one, is red ; and Roma, the right one, white. The veins were supposed to contain air.—Cf. *Jaeschke*, p. 436.

that will beset him by the way and gives him the names of the men with stag-heads and dog-heads and tells him not to be afraid. If Obame refuses his prayer to enter Dewajen, and he cannot reach another paradise, then he should try and come back to Man's Country and reincarnate as a man—not as a woman, as she is only "half a man" (miluchega), being unable to be a king or an official, and always under the rule of a husband. The man chosen for father should be humble, peaceful, kindly, lucky, rich. With the knowledge obtained from the lama, the spirit should be able to come back as a man; if he is a good man, and listens to the lama, he will have this knowledge; but if he has been bad in this life, he will not think of anything else except incarnation, and he may come back as a dog or other animal.

Then the Podeb pulls a few hairs on the front part of the head of the corpse, and draws the spirit out through the head and sends it to Dewajen. He can tell whether the spirit has come out by a minute swelling (jewo tsang bug), on the front of the head, from which yellow water issues. If the swelling is so soft that one can stick a blade of grass (dsa-kusha) in it, everything is well.

Before this feat of sending the spirit to Dewajen can be accomplished successfully, not only must the Podeb be very powerful and good, but the deceased also must have been a very good man. For only very good men have an aperture at the junction of the frontal and parietal bones. If the aperture is at the back of the skull, like that one on your book-shelf, it means that the man has not been particularly good. If there is no aperture at all, the man must have been thoroughly bad, and his spirit cannot be drawn out in this way. Hence the saying: "Lama-la dren be jag ju yö na, lhoma la de be a-lung me na, drin ba mi nü," that is, "The lama may have a hook, but if the spirit has no ring, he cannot hook it up."

When a man dies, his spirit is asleep until two hours before noon on the third day. For instance, if he dies on Saturday morning, his spirit wakes up at ten o'clock on Monday morning, and it may roam about until forty-nine days after death. During these forty-nine days it is customary to burn a little tsamba and butter and tiny pieces of cloth, as the spirit can smell this offering, and to pour tea from his tsamba bowl on the floor round the fire. Beer is not offered. His bowl is kept beside the Podeb.*

"On the third day the spirit wakes up and says to himself: What is wrong with me? What have I done? Then he will think—Maybe I dead! He imagines he has a body like a living man but is afraid. He goes into the room where the family is sitting at a meal and looks to see whether a place is left for him. He sees his tsamba bowl beside the lama and all the people are crying, very sorry. He is afraid he is dead, and goes up to the roof to see whether he has a shadow. There is none. He goes down to the river side and walks on the sand; he leaves no footprints. Then he knows for sure that he is dead, and he returns and tries to get into his body again but cannot; it is cold—like earth or stone. In despair he searches for a husband and

* Waddell (*Lamaism*, p. 491) says that the deceased is always at every meal offered his share of what is going, including tobacco, etc., up to the 49th day from death. Sherap says that this may be a Sikhim custom, but it is not Tibetan, that is, it does not exist between Shigatse and Dartsendo.

wife in conjugal embrace and endeavours to enter the womb but cannot, because he has not been before the King of Hell and purged of sin. It is no use.

"So he will try to find out the way that the lama spoke of and sets out along the Bardo Trong, the road that lies between death and rebirth. He forgets the lama's words and has no power, just as if blown by the wind. He follows a road bordered with trees and flowers, very beautiful, but leading nowhere. He comes back and wanders to many places and is chased by many men who have not human heads but animals' heads of all kinds, and all these people have swords and spears and bows and lassoes. It is cold, dark, dreadful, sorrowful. If knowledgeful and good, he is not afraid ; he thinks it all a dream ; he knows he has no body and must find the way.

"Now, although the lama had told the spirit that he must go direct to Dewajen and ask to be let in, and if refused try some other paradise, and, if unsuccessful still, return to Man's Country—although he told him all this and never said that first he must go before the King of Hell, yet every spirit, whether good or bad, must first go to Nyalwa and appear before the King. So at last the creatures with the lassoes catch him and lead him away.*

"Then, bound by the lasso, he kneels in front of Shinje Chöjel ; and beside him are two devil-like creatures with a large pair of scales, one of whom tells his good deeds in the world and the other his evil. For each good deed a white pebble (diugar) is put in one scale, and for each evil deed a black pebble (diunag) is put in the other. When they have

* Although so terrifying in appearance, they are not devils but small deities who serve the King of Hell and bring to him for examination any man they find wandering on Bardo Trong. They are called Zhitro, Damba, Rigja.

finished, the King says "Bring me the scales (garnag jama)!" and he examines them; then, "Bring me the mirror of good and bad deeds (gedig melong)!" and he compares what it shows with the results of the scales; then, "Bring me the Tramshing!" and he inspects the marks on the wooden board. Then he gives judgment. If the white pebbles are very heavy and the black very light, and the melong and tramshing give the same result, the King will say that the spirit may go to Dewajen Zhinkam.* On hearing this, the spirit is like a man released from prison, dancing, singing, very glad. He remembers the lȧma who taught him, and he calls him to come with all the lamas of that sect who had helped him, and they come and lead him to Dewajen.

"When the spirit reaches Dewajen, although he has no body, he can get one from the lotus, just as a flower comes from the seed. Many other spirits are there—all kindful; they do not know about anger, trouble, lust, jealousy. It is not as in Man's Country —this mine, that yours. There are no mountains or rocks in the Dewajen country; it is full of flowers, and all kinds of sweet sounds of birds singing. All the time they can see Obame's face. He has Chana Dorje on his right hand and Janrezig on his left—very bright and beautiful. When all the spirits see their faces, all are very happy, and they live there for ever.

"It is not always to Dewajen that the King of Hell sends good spirits. There are many paradises to which a good spirit may go, such as Yulogobe Zhinkam, Shambala, Kajö Zhinkam, and other smaller ones. Great lamas who are very good do

* Zhinkam means "happy land."

not go to any of these paradises but to Nirvana; and some deny themselves Nirvana and come back reincarnated (drulgu) into Man's Country in order to try to save all sinners.

"Should the King of Hell find that the black and white pebbles weigh about the same, or even the black be a little heavier, he will say to the spirit: "You did not do very wrong, but you must go back to Man's Country. You must live a better life than before and do more good deeds. You must believe in Buddha's dharma, and listen to the lama's words, and do kindfully. Afterwards you may get to Dewajen." The King also advises him to reincarnate as a man rather than as a woman, but the spirit has no control over that.

"So the spirit goes back to Man's Country, and, if he is very knowledgeful, he will look out for a husband and wife who are good, lucky, rich, and of high position, because all these qualities will assist him in acquiring merit by doing good deeds. Now, it is as difficult to find a good man 'as a star in the daytime'—*nyin möi gar ma dra ba*; but, if he is fortunate and finds such a pair, he will seize the chance to enter once more on the Wheel of Life."

If the spirit is a sinner he will not go back to Man's Country. Murderers and robbers are sent to Nyalwa, where they suffer for a long time before being set free. Rich people who are miserly (selna) and have not given to the poor, and have prized money so much that they were loth to spend it even on food for themselves, are sent to Yidag, the Hunger Country. These are people who, unlike the Dre, when about to die are afraid, and wonder what will be their lot in the next world. In the Yidag country they see plenty of food, but archers and spearmen prevent them from reaching it. While in this world they disliked spending money, even on eating and drinking, so now they have a fire in the mouth (yidag kalamebar). They have a big stomach and thin legs; their throat is so small that it cannot take sufficient food to satisfy the stomach, and even if the stomach did receive food, their legs would be too weak to support it.

Those spirits who, when in the world, were stupid, lazy, without knowledge, go to the Animals' Country (Düdro or Jösong), which is very little better than Yidag. The Lhamayin country is where they send men who have always been short-tempered and abusive in this world; the Lhamayin wear soldiers' dress and carry arms and are always fighting, just as when they were in Man's Country.

Those whose only aim in this world was pleasure, leading good lives and doing no wrong, but never doing good works, caring nothing for the next world, are sent to the Lha Country, where they live a very long time amidst all sorts of pleasure. In Lha are beautiful gardens, with every kind of sweet-smelling flower, and garlands retain their scent and do not wither for a whole year or more. The walls of the houses are full of precious things, the chairs are studded with precious stones and have very soft seats, and all the time beautiful girls, lhamo (Ch. hsien nü), play on the biwang. But one day a Lha hears a voice from heaven (Namka) saying: "After seven days you will die," and he has no more peace in his heart. At once his garlands begin to wither and his body to become offensive, and his friends lead him to the Lha country's *durtro* to spend his seven days.

There they leave him, saying: "You are going to die now, but perhaps you will come back to us." The seven days appear like seven hundred years. He is alone, cold, hungry, sorrowful, friendless, suffering all kinds of evils, and he cannot die. However, he dies at last and goes before the King of Hell; but, as he may be without knowledge, he may be reincarnated as a man or as an animal.

This is the teaching of Hinayana, that through knowledge you may escape from the Wheel of Life, but without it you will continue in the cycle of transmigration; for without knowledge you cannot do good deeds; and it takes nine good lives to qualify for Dewajen. The Geluba, or Established Church, believe in this theory, and take no great count of the Guru Pedma Sambhava. On the other hand the Nyima, or Unreformed sect, hold the Mahayana doctrine—that the spirit of a dead person is in the same position as a snake inside a bamboo stem; it must go either up or down, there is no alternative; that is, it either goes straight to paradise or straight to hell. The Sachyaba also hold to this belief, while the Karjuba have what the Chinese call a "hua chiao," a mixed or piebald religion, believing both. The sub-sect Düba has a creed which has been compared to a thread composed of black and white strands twisted in combination. Like the Karjuba, the modern Bönbo creed is a mixture, but largely Mahayana.

The Kangjur relates how Buddha's cousin, Jungdsega, was much in love with a very beautiful girl named Pandárika, who had an equal affection for him. They lived so happily together that they could not bear to be parted from each other for a moment. However, one day Buddha succeeded in leading his cousin out for a walk and exhorted him to give up Pandárika, but without success. Seeing a blind monkey on the road, Buddha enquired of his cousin, "Which do you think the more beautiful, the monkey or Pandárika ?" "Pandárika, of course," replied Jungdsega, "she is as lovely as a flower." "Very well," said Buddha, "I shall show you something more beautiful," and he directed him along a road which took him to the Lha country. There in a garden of exquisite loveliness were the most entrancing female forms that he had ever beheld ; all was gay and fair, and the seats were thrones studded with jewels. One of these thrones was empty, and Jungdsega, enquiring to whom it belonged, was informed that it was for Buddha's cousin, who was expected presently. "I am Buddha's cousin," said Jungdsega, but they did not believe him, because he was still a man. So, hastening back to Buddha, he pleaded to be allowed to go to the Lha country. "But what of Pandárika ?" enquired Buddha. "Pandárika," was the reply, "compared with the Lhamo is like that blind monkey." "Very well," said Buddha, "but first you must see another country," and he directed him along a road which led to Hell. There Jungdsega saw men being sliced in pieces and others being boiled in great pots. One of these cauldrons was empty, and asking for whom it was intended, Jungdsega was told that it was for Buddha's cousin, who was expected presently ; that once he had given a bowl of rice to Buddha and he was, therefore, being sent to the Lha country for seven days, but after that he was coming to Hell. Just then Jungdsega observed a number of bowmen and men with lassoes looking up expectantly to Man's country and, very frightened, he hastened back to Buddha and penitently said that he no longer wished to go to the Lha country, and pleaded to be saved from Hell. Buddha replied, "Very well; but you must follow my teaching and obey my law." And this he did so faithfully that in course of time he became the chief of the five hundred drajomba who attained Nirvana.

CHAPTER VIII

ON BURIAL CUSTOMS.

Four Methods of Burial—Duke Yo's Artfulness—Exposure to the Eagles—Burial in the Ground—Thrown in River—Cremation—Chöden and Tsa-Tsa—Embalmed Lamas.

WHEN anyone dies, a soothsayer is called in to fix the date of burial, which should be within seven days of death, and to decide in which of the four ways the corpse should be buried—whether by heaven, or by fire, or by water, or by earth. This he does after comparing the element-animal combinations of the birth and death years and consulting his books.

Burial by heaven is effected by exposing the body to the eagles ; this is the method commonly used in the case of all ordinary persons that have died a natural death, including lamas of the lesser ranks. In burial by water the body is generally sewn in a skin and thrown in the river, a method practised in the case of paupers or such as have died of leprosy. Those who have died of small-pox or similar contagious or infectious disease, instead of being thrown in the river, may be buried in the ground. Cremation is reserved for great lamas and high officials.

The celebrated Chinese General Yo Kungyeh,* is credited in popular tradition with the introduction of the custom of exposure to the eagles. Finding that in Tibet were many of those localities known to the Chinese as "Lung Mo Ti," places of the

* Duke Yo (Yo Chung-ch 'i), a native of Kansu, A.D. 1686–1754. Expedition against Tibet, 1719–20.—Giles, *Biog. Dict.*, Art. 2,500.

dragon's pulse,* and recognising that burial in such spots would bring great luck to the family of the deceased—his sons or grandsons perhaps producing a great general or king who might conquer China—Duke Yo persuaded the Tibetans that they might do much better than bury their dead in the ground. The argument he used was that, when so buried, the dead are of no use to anyone; whereas, if given to the hungry birds, the givers would reap the reward merited by good works. That is how the practice started, which is now the commonest method of burial in Tibet.† In Dartsendo itself cremation and burial in the earth are the forms in vogue; but westward from Mi-nyag, three days out along the south road, and from Gada, four days along the north road, the practice of exposure to the eagles is universal except among nomads. And it is not so long since it was common in Dartsendo; outside the south gate, at the foot of a hill near the bridge, is the old durtro, or place of burial, in this case a large flat rock on which the bodies were exposed. Among nomads the custom is confined to the rich: in general, the body is simply taken about three miles away from the camp, dumped there and left.

* Dr. Giles, in his Dictionary, interprets Lung Mo (meaning literally "dragon's pulse" or "dragon's arteries") as "magnetic currents recognised by geomancers as influencing the fortunes of places, families, etc." Williams, in his *Middle Kingdom*, says: "The principles of geomancy depend much on two supposed currents running through the earth, known as the dragon and the tiger; a propitious site has these on its left and right. Burial-places are selected by geomancers, and their location has important results on the prosperity of the living."—Vol. II, pp. 245–6.

† Rockhill suggests that the reason for the preference of the form of obsequies known as "celestial interment" lies in the lamaist theory of the "intermediate state" (bardo) between death and regeneration, which it is most desirable to shorten. Its length depends on the time requisite for the complete dissolution of the body, which here means its digestion by the birds, dogs, or fishes; and the birds do it most quickly.—*L. of L.*, p. 16, note.

Tied up with knees to chin, and wrapped in a gown which completely covers it, the corpse to be exposed is loaded on one side of a horse, a basket of stones balancing it on the other, and thus carried to the durtro. There it is stripped, its limbs pulled straight, and laid face downward, the head wrapped in a cloth. In order to induce the eagles to eat it, it is necessary that it should be cut up ; and it is advisable to have it lying on its face because otherwise, with the first cuts on the breast, reflex movements of the muscles would frighten those cutting. The latter are the friends of the deceased, perhaps ten or twenty in number, and they make the cuts in the swastika pattern, commencing from the shoulder blades.

When the cutting is finished, a Jöba lama reads and prays, beats a drum and blows a thigh-bone trumpet. Sometimes the eagles, guided by the behaviour of a black eagle, their king, do not come to this invitation but circle round and round. If the black eagle does not eat, the others also refuse, and this indicates to the Jöba that the deceased must have been a sinner. In order, therefore, to induce the eagles to feed, the Jöba, with knife and hook, cuts himself a piece of the flesh and eats it. Thereupon the king-eagle swoops down and feeds, and all the rest follow his example. The friends sit by, drinking tea and beer, and watch the body being eaten, which does not take long, perhaps about an hour. When only the bones are left, they come forward and break them with stones into a powder, which they mix with tsamba and give to the eagles. Finally they pound the head with stones, mix in some tsamba, so as to form a sort of meat balls, and feed these also to the eagles. Then all go home.

In Lhasa, although the body is tied up and covered in the same way as elsewhere, it is carried to the durtro on the back of a lama called the Tobden. It is the Tobden also, not the friends, who cuts the body and pounds the bones and head.

Burial in the ground is reserved for persons that have died from some highly infectious or contagious disease of the nature of small-pox or virulent fevers; it is believed that the earth will prevent the disease from spreading and making others sick. In this method of burial coffins are not used, although children are often buried in a wooden bucket, or earthenware pot, or tea-basket. The place of burial, dursa or durkung, is chosen by the soothsayer, who attends the funeral and reads books; and sometimes a lama also is present. Usually the friends of the deceased are afraid to touch the corpse themselves and, for the burial, employ "low men, never-mind men." No stone or mound marks the place. When the grave is filled in, the surface is smoothed flat and turf placed on top, so that the spot may not be distinguishable. Before Duke Yo's time this was the ordinary method of burial in Tibet, and, owing to Chinese influence, it survives in Dartsendo, where the Chinese form of burial, with mound and stones, is carried out with even slightly greater elaboration than is usual in China.

Burial by water is the form held in least esteem: it is generally confined to lepers, beggars, and babies. Lepers are first sewn in skins, but beggars are thrown in the river without this formality; and sometimes the same fate falls to rich men who have been robbed and murdered in lonely places. Babies are put in a basket, which is not weighted. On such occasions the soothsayer does not attend, because in the case of beggars there is no one to pay his fee, and in the case of a baby no one cares, even a male baby being regarded "all same little piece of mud." If a soothsayer, called in to decide on the method of burial, gives the verdict of burial by water, all the family begin to cry and say, "Please not throw in water," but he explains: "If not throw in water, very bad luck for family," so they are obliged to acquiesce.

Cremation is reserved for lamas of the higher ranks—ngambu, durgu, geshi—and persons with a reputation for wisdom. At death the corpse is bathed with saffron water (the only occasion on which a body is washed before burial), and the trunk, arms, and legs separately bound round with white cotton cloth. Dressed in its best, it is made to sit tailor-fashion on a rug with the hands in one of two positions, (1) the right hand lying in the palm of the left (Ti. Nyamshak), or (2) the right hand stretched out, the left held palm upward against the abdomen (Ti. Sanön Nyamshak). Over the head and face a kada is lightly laid, and on the head is placed the hat characteristic of the sect. Round the corpse on the floor are low tables with many butter lamps, 100 or 1,000, according to the wealth of the deceased, and a few baptismal bottles filled with saffron water.

The death-chamber, whether in a lamasery or outside of it, is filled with lamas; and every day until the corpse is cremated the lama of highest rank will read books and wash away the sins of the deceased, from a baptismal vase in his right hand pouring saffron water on a round brass melong in his left.

A site having been carefully chosen, a chöden is built on it and whitewashed; it has four doors, facing exactly north, south, east, and west, opening into the oven, which is just large enough to take the body. In the oven is a bar of iron, laid horizontally. The body is then brought to the chöden on a sort of small table made fast over a carrying-pole, borne usually by four bearers. Tibetans do not trouble about the number of bearers, as the Chinese do. On arrival at the chöden, the pole is detached and the legs of the corpse pulled straight with much difficulty and a cracking noise. The body is then put inside the oven, astride the iron bar, in the position of a rider. Lamas are present from all the four sects—Geluba, Sachyaba, Nyimaba, Karjuba—irrespective of the particular sect of the deceased; the Bönbo are not represented. The chief lamas of the various sects have each a stick wrapped in cloth full of butter, and butter is also put on the firewood under the iron bar. The lamas are not arranged according to sect in any particular position, north, south, east, or west, round the chöden. They all read simultaneously different passages from the scriptures, and then the four representative lamas light their torches and apply them to the firewood.

When the body is completely burned, the bones, which break easily in the hand like charcoal, are taken to the lamasery and mixed with mud. From this compound are moulded several thousand miniature chöden (tsa-tsa), which are preserved in a large whitewashed chöden built of mud and stone outside the lamasery. The temporary chöden in which the body was cremated is destroyed.

The very highest lamas, such as the Dalai and

the Panchen, are not cremated but embalmed. Their chöden are made of copper, gold-washed, and decorated with precious stones, and butter-lamps are lighted before them daily by the lamas.

The embalmed bodies of the Dalai lamas are preserved at Potala, and those of the Panchen lamas at Drashilhunbo. Tsongkaba was also embalmed and is kept at Galden.

CHAPTER IX

THE NOMADS—DROGBA.

The Tent—Their Dress—" Day after Day "—Names of Tribes—The Wild Golok—Raw Meat—A Milking Custom—Za and Genema—Die in their Boots—The Great Robbing Expedition—The Drung Hunt—Marriage by Capture—Stag, Muskdeer, Badger, and Fox—A Notable Robber—Nagchuka—Nagtsang—Sheep as Transport—Snaring the Wild Horse—The Dalai Lama's Preserve—Droshü—Janyima Fair.

THE nomads live in tents of a fabric woven of black yak hair. As each family possesses a great number of animals requiring pasturage, the tents are usually pitched several miles apart : only in exceptional cases are three or four found together.

The large Golok tent, which is the typical nomad tent, is of oblong shape, like a foreign loaf, and is made in two parts so that, when these are put together, an opening is left lengthwise down the middle of the roof, which serves the double purpose of letting in the light and letting out smoke. At night time this opening can be covered by a flap of yak-hair cloth. Poles at either end support the roof of the tent, and if it is a very large one, an additional pole is placed in the middle. The door is at one end. The pole farthest from the door carries a prayer flag, and if the owner is rich the tent pegs also have flags. Small tents are square in shape.

Entering one of these tents you see a chöba set against the opposite wall, that is to say, a long, narrow table on which stand brass bowls full of water, behind which are butter lamps always alight, and behind the butter lamps the idols. Above the table are ranged various books of scripture, parts of the Kangjur and Denjur.* The left-hand side of the tent, looking from the door, is reserved for the women, and here are kept the cooking utensils and the food. The right-hand side is reserved for the men ; there are stacked the weapons and boxes of such valuables as the family possesses. Men and women keep each to their own side of the tent at night-time, sleeping on yak-skins with a felt over them and a saddle for pillow. In the middle of the floor is the stove made of mud, round which, when they want to sit, they spread yak-skins on the ground.

Rich families have sometimes several small tents in addition to the large one. Even the poor family, living in one small tent, has its idols and butter lamps and its sacred books, which visiting lamas read aloud. Many of the lamaseries are just encampments, the great tent in the middle being used as the temple.

Summer and winter alike, the typical nomad dress for both sexes is a sheepskin coat with the wool inside. It takes five or six skins to make a coat. Men's sheepskins are edged with black or red Chinese cloth, and a leopard skin is thrown round the neck and sometimes across one breast. Women's sheepskins are edged with cloth of three colours : black, red, and green, in rows ; they do not wear the leopard skin. Unless they are rich, in which case they may wear a cotton shirt and perhaps a cotton or woollen petticoat, this sheepskin, tied round the middle, is all the nomad woman's costume, except for boots and cap. Both men and women wear long boots of

* The Canon and the Commentaries.

calf-skin with the hair inside. Some nomad tribes, however, whom I shall mention by and by, dress in the Tibetan style.

In winter the nomads remain camped at their headquarters, but at the approach of summer they lead out their cattle to seek pasturage, and in this pursuit move about from place to place for several months, taking their smaller tents with them, the big ones being left behind in charge of the old members of the family, along with the children and lamas. During this leisurely movement from place to place one day is very much like another. Just before sunrise the yaks, which, in obedience to some instinct, never stray far from the camp at night, are sent up the mountain to graze. About daybreak the nomad gets up, rubs his eyes, and may or may not trouble to wash. If he does, the process consists in taking a mouthful of water from his tsamba bowl, blowing it out on his hands, and so rinsing them. Some take a second mouthful, which they blow on their hands and then rub on their faces. They do not bathe the body at all, and are a healthy people with few diseases; in Dsachuka I saw many old persons of 80 or 90, and one or two were said to be 100 years of age.

Up so early, the nomad prepares a chota-hazri of tea, with a little tsamba. In this respect he is like the ordinary Tibetan who believes that, when the stomach is empty, as for example the first thing in the morning or after a long and tiring journey, water rises from the liver which should be pressed down again by taking a mouthful of food. This snack is called "chin-nön," literally "liver-pressing."

An hour or so after sunrise the work of the day

begins. A woman comes out of the tent and calls the yak to be milked. A man having a journey to make comes out with a lasso and catches his horse; another lassoes a yak, to be cut up for meat. Most of them employ themselves in hunting, making belts, leather, ropes, repairing the tent or, if it is early summer, shearing the sheep; while the women are busy making butter, curds, tsamba, etc. About 10 a.m., after the yak have been milked, all breakfast together off tea, tsamba, curds, cheese, yak meat, or mutton. Then the small boys, from ten to fifteen years of age, take the yak out for the day, carrying with them bags of tea and tsamba, and a sling with which to stone straying yaks. Often the wind is so violent that it carries the pebbles with it, and the tsamba in your bowl is blown in your face. At the camp, dinner is about 2 p.m., and is the same as breakfast. Nomads have no beer or spirits and as they do not keep pigs, they have no pork, neither have they vegetables. Before sunset the boys bring the yak home, and when milking is over, all squat down to supper by the light of butter lamps. Round the stove after supper they tell stories, sing, talk nonsense, and are quite happy. Then comes the recital from memory of prayers to Drölma, Goddess of Mercy. Before turning in, each person kneels three times before the idols and prays; and after lying down, those who are not sleepy may talk about the stars, many of which they know by name. In summer it often rains; nomads look forward to the winter when, if it is not snowing, they can all sleep outside under the stars, for they do not fear the cold.

The following are the nomad tribes and countries,

beginning in the north-east and proceeding south-west towards India. From the Golok, who are an independent nation, going west you come to Dsachuka, which is under both Derge and Kansu, and west of that, through wild country, to Dsagarnag, or Gedse Dsagarnag, and Adra Dsamar, both of which countries are under the Nangchen Jelbo or king. Thence you pass through the Dam country and enter North Nagchuka. Southward of this is a big lake called Nam,* round which live the Namruma, the Tent People of Nam, beyond whom is the great snow range called Nyen Chen Tang La. South of this range is Bangba Bayang, and turning west you come to Yangbachen and to the two Nagtsang, Lower and Upper. North-west of them is Bangba Chugdso, a poor country with a great snow mountain called Dargo, and a great turquoise lake, Dangra. South of Mount Dargo is Yönchödengga, a nomad country with a few houses. Farther west lie Lower and Upper Droshü, with the Soda Lake, and Gedse-jangba, famous for salt. Then comes the big pass, called Mayum La, and beyond it Lake Mapam, both in nomad country. North of these is a country called Barka Dazam, between which and India are the wild lands of Janyima and Jakargo, where in summer Indians and Tibetans camp and trade. West of these is Dretaburi, the last nomad country.

Now I shall describe briefly these places as I saw them ; and I saw all except the Golok. But I have a good deal to say of the Golok, learned from one of that country named Gelo, who stayed for a year in my compound in Dartsendo, and from Pedma

* Tengri Nor.

Rinchen, who had lived among them for about two years.*

The Golok country is divided into five districts, each governed by an official called Bön. Their dialect (drog-ge, "nomad talk") and that of Dsachuka are very much the same, and these two have also many customs in common. All five districts are very cold and wild, with great sandy plains, bare of trees and good grass, with no houses, only tents of black yak hair.

The Goloks live on yak, mutton, butter, milk, cheese, and sour milk, also a little tsamba, which they get from Amdo and Sungpan. They have an unusual method of killing cattle for food, by tying a leather rope tightly round the nose and mouth until the eyes protrude and the animal dies of suffocation, the process taking nearly half an hour. Sometimes when a yak is killed, they eat the meat raw and still warm, and drink the warm blood, making a cup of both hands; this is not a universal custom. A sheep slaughtered for food lasts ten persons two days. When the women find that the yaks are not giving milk, they apply their mouths to the vulva and blow, with the object of distending the animal's stomach and causing the milk to come;

* "The Golok are the most interesting but unfortunately the least known of the tribes of northern Tibet."—Rockhill, *L. of L.*, p. 188.

" The Chinese have never exercised any control over the nomads of the grass-lands north of the Yalung valley above Kanze, which extend from here east to Sungpan in Szechuan and north across the Yellow river basin to Taochou and Labrang Gomba in Kansu. This vast extent of country is inhabited by the Golok and other wild nomad tribes, and, being a closed land to Chinese and foreigners, remains one of the least known parts of Asia. It is enclosed in a rough triangle formed by the following three caravan routes: Tachienlu-Kanze-Jyekundo, Jyekundo-Sining, Sining-Taochou-Sungpan-Tachienlu; all these roads are subject to raids from the nomads living inside the triangle they enclose. The Golokwa appear to recognise the temporal authority of the Lhasa Tibetans as little as they do that of the Chinese."—*Teichman*, p. 77.

this custom is common all over Tibet, but in some places the women use a tube.

Costume is similar to that of other nomads, except that the head-dress, rings, and ear-rings are a little different. Both men and women wear caps of lambskin, with the wool inside, the men's caps being conical and the women's pie-shaped. All wear ear-rings, the men's annular and the women's pendant and of considerable length. Women wear the hair hanging down in plaits, of which there are many, and have amber, coral, and turquoise ornaments on the head, and necklaces of coloured glass or, in the case of rich persons, coral and turquoise. Among the Golok a family is accounted rich if it possess 1,000 yak, 2,000–3,000 sheep, 100–200 horses; a poor family has only 20–30 yak, 300–400 sheep, 10–20 horses; and very poor persons, who have no property at all, are servants to the rich.

Rich and poor, old and young, male and female, the Golok all like to have the lama come and read the scriptures to them. To lamas visiting the country they are liberal with gifts. High officials and kings' sons they will rob without a qualm, but they will not rob a lama. Only two sects are represented, the Geluba and the Nyimaba. They are more afraid of the Nyimaba than of the Geluba, and sometimes desperate characters will attack a yellow sect lama,* because his chöjong are generally milder

* In April, 1918, Mr. Teichman was eye-witness of a Golok raid on Sershu monastery. "The Golokwa, being by all accounts very religious, had no business to be raiding the stock of a monastery; but it appears that they belong almost entirely to the old unreformed red sects, and have not a proper respect for a Gelugba establishment. But the lamas said that they expect to get their stock back after negotiation and payment of presents, when it had been established that the ponies belonged to them and not to laymen."—*Teich.*, p. 93.

Père Huc relates the murder, by Goloks, in 1841, of a Kanbo legate sent by the Dalai Lama to the Court at Peking.—*Souvenirs* II, 181.

than those of the Nyima, which has a very fierce tutelary called Za, with nine heads and eyes all over his body, and another, a demoness tutelary, called Lhamo Genema, in Sanskrit Ekadsati,* who has one eye and one tooth, and one short queue standing up on the front of the head like that of a Chinese infant. The Golok make nothing of robbery and murder, although they constantly pray to The Three Holy Ones. If a man dies peacefully and naturally on his nyesa (mattress), they regard him as a useless weakling who has come to a dishonourable end. One who has killed many men and is at last himself killed by sword, spear, or rifle, is looked upon with esteem and is said to have done well.

The Golok are all robbers. Their chief weapon used to be the long Golok lance, "Golok dung-ring," which was six feet in length, its shaft bound round with wire to turn the edge of a sword, and decked with a piece of red cloth near the blade ; but nowadays they have plenty of Russian rifles. Every year the Golok, in different parts of their country, to the number of one or two hundred families in each gathering, say between three and seven hundred persons, male and female, meet together to discuss a suitable date for starting on the Lojag, the annual robbing expedition. On this adventure men take their wives and such of their children as can sit a horse, and they travel great distances, often for one month outward, while old persons and infants

* Ekadsati: Waddell quotes a legend that when Pedma Samdhava was warring against the local devils of Tibet, the white fiendess, Ekadsati, showered thunderbolts on him and he retaliated by melting her snow-dwelling into a lake, which he then caused to boil. Although all her flesh was boiled off, she did not emerge, so he threw in his thunderbolt, piercing her right eye. Then she came forth and made submission.—*Wadd.*, p. 384, n. 1.

are left at home, it may be to suffer at the hands of other Golok robbers. Should such predatory bands meet on the road, they do not molest each other. On the return of the expedition, if it has been successful, the spoil is divided among the families engaged, in proportion to the number of persons in each family. If unsuccessful, there is nothing for it but to kill and eat the horses.

A similar annual excursion takes place in autumn, this time in pursuit of the wild yak, or Drung, an animal almost as big as the elephant, that lives in herds of one or two hundred all over the northern nomad country, but mostly in Golok and Dsachuka.* The same number of persons engage in this great hunt as in the robber raid. When living with the herd, the drung is not very fierce ; but if solitary, he is a man-killer : one lick of his rough tongue strips the flesh off a man's arm. Goloks tell of seeing drung with a man's skeleton on its horns. Sometimes, they say, when it gores a man, it is unable to disentangle his body from its horns or throw him off, and so wanders about while the flesh gradually rots from the man's carcase and only the skeleton is left, still inextricably attached. This is what the Goloks tell, but I have not seen it. When they have a kill, they eat the drung's heart while still warm and palpitating, in the belief that it imparts courage.

Marriage by capture has already been described. When a Golok steals a girl in his own country, he takes her to another Golok country, where he

* "There are also found wild oxen, very near as big as elephants, very fair, having white and black hair, short in other parts, and on the shoulder three palms, long, fine, white, and in many respects beyond silk, of which hair our author brought some to Venice."—*Marco Polo*, ch. 14.

makes submission to the chief, who gives him protection ; or, he may steal a girl from another Golok country and bring her home, where he is protected ; or, he leaves the Golok altogether and takes her to Dsachuka, but he never takes her to a warm country, as the Golok are accustomed to great cold and do not like warm countries. Similarly, Dsachuka and Derge men bring girls they capture to Golok, for Golok and Dsachuka are safe places for them. The Golok are monogamous. Perhaps half of them are married in the ordinary Tibetan style : the other half do not go through any ceremony, and of these a considerable proportion have captured their brides.

That is all I have to say about the Golok.

Dsachuka is the region of the Dsachu, or Upper Yalung, and is divided in jurisdiction between Derge and Kansu and governed by Bön, or hereditary chiefs, of whom there are several. Kansu does not interfere with the Government, leaving it in the hands of the Bön, who, however, must pay a tax annually to the Kansu official at Jyekundo. Similarly, the portion under Derge is administered by its own Bön, who pay a tax to the Jelbo at Derge Gonchen. It is not such a wild country as Golok : in summer its grassy plains are beautiful with flowers. Its people live in tents, dress like the Goloks, practise monogamy, and otherwise, especially in the north, assimilate to the Golok : in the south they are more like the Derge people. Each year in autumn they are visited by three caravans, one from Derge, one from Denko, and one from Kanze, so that they are better supplied with tsamba than are the Golok. Their lamaseries are mostly small ones of the Nyima sect, but there is a large Geluba lamasery at Sershu. In Golok and Dsachuka you find the wealthiest of the nomads.

Next we come to the Nangchen Jelbo's territory, lying south-west of Jyekundo, and comprising two small countries, of which the northern portions are inhabited by nomads, namely Dsagarnag and Adra Dsamar, also called Adra Meimar ; the southern portions being farm land. Dsagarnag adjoins Dsachuka and, in its northern part, is a poor country, with very few trees, governed by a Bön known as the Gedse Bön. Its people live chiefly by hunting. In spring and summer such as possess rifles and horses hunt the stag. In the second or third Chinese moon, say about March–April, the stag's horns bleed ; and there is a great demand in China for the bleeding horns, which are regarded as a strengthening medicine and fetch over Tls. 100 a pair.* In winter time they snare the muskdeer, sending the musk to the Jyekundo market. Poor persons hunt the badger and the fox with sticks and dogs, the badger in summer, the fox in autumn, employing the winter in trading the fox-skins ; there is nothing for them to do in spring except to go after badger in their burrows, not an easy business, as they go so deep. The fox is not the real fox, but an inferior animal called *Be* in Tibetan, and *Sha-hu* in Chinese, whose skin fetches not more than three or four rupees.† The badger is called *Chü-wa* in Tibetan and *t'u-t'u-tzu* in Chinese : it is hunted both for its skin and for food. The skin is not traded, but made into garments : the flesh is almost as fat as pork. The

* Tael, a Chinese weight : an ounce (of silver), say 3/-.

† Fox : Giles, in his Chinese Dictionary, calls it the "corsac, or fox of the steppes."

people of Dsagarnag dress like Tibetans, but the men wear ornaments in their hair, which is not a common practice in Tibet. Unlike the Golok and Dsachuka peoples, the men have queues, and their customs vary much among themselves. Their lamaseries are mostly of the Karju sect.

Adjoining Dsagarnag, and west of it, is Adra Dsamar, also a small country, not quite so poor as the former, but otherwise much the same, and governed by a Bön known as the Adra Bön. The people are poorly clad and robbers abound. When I was there about twenty years ago, the country was being terrorised by a robber chief styled Gedmo Dagjel, who wore princely clothes and had a following of about 100 men, all splendidly dressed, well mounted, and properly equipped with guns and tents. Adra Dsamar is all rocky hills and grassy plains, but the grass is poor, and, as in Dsagarnag, the people live chiefly by hunting, dwelling in yak-hair tents and wearing sheepskin coats. They also use a coarse white Tibetan woollen cloth, nambu, called *mu-tzu* in Chinese, a long coat of which costs ten rupees.

Passing through the small nomad country of Dam, or Damjashog, rich in yaks and horses, we come next to Chang Nagchuka, the North Black-River country. It is a fine nomad country. Nagchuka and Dam send yak, sheep, dried beef, butter, and cheese to Lhasa, which is seven or eight days journey to the south, and bring back wheat, rice, cloth, etc. Caravans from Jyekundo bound for Lhasa generally unload in Dam or Nagchuka and there hire local carriers to transport their merchandise to the capital, thus affording their own animals a good rest. There are no large monasteries, but all the sects are represented. The Nagchuka people and the Damba dress in the Tibetan style, and, although not so rich as some of the Golok and Dsachuka nomads, they are very prosperous, and are as well off as any nomad country in respect of the ordinary comforts of life.

Round Lake Nam are the Namruma, covering an area as large as Nagchuka. At Lake Nam are only a few small lamaseries, but at the foot of the snow range, Nyen Chen Tang La, are several of importance ; and on the other side of it is Dalung (tiger) Monastery, with a hutuktu called Marinboje and, a little to the east, Redring Gomba, near which are many juniper trees.*

Bangba Bayang is a very small country of only one or two hundred nomad families. It has many lakes, visited by thousands of duck. I lived there in Headman Wednesday's tent for two months. In custom and manner of living the Bayang people resemble those of Nagchuka and the Damba. Annually in the autumn they go down to Dölung Tsurbu lamasery and trade their yak, sheep, and dried meat for wheat and barley. This lamasery is the biggest of the Karju sect, housing about four hundred lamas, and has a great temple with many big idols in it. It was founded by Karmaba, whose reincarnation lives there, and it is about one day's journey north of Lhasa.†

*Redring : " To the North East of Lhasa was the first lamasery of Reformed Lamaism. It was founded by Atisha's chief Tibetan disciple, Bromton, in 1058 A.D."—*Wadd.*, p. 56.

† The Karmaba sub-sect of the Karjuba was founded by Karmaba in the middle of the twelfth century ; and the monastery built in 1154 at Tsurbu, about one day's journey to the north of Lhasa, is still the headquarters of this the most powerful of all the Karjuba sub-sects."—*Wadd.*, p. 67.

North-west of Dölung Tsurbu and close to it is another very small nomad country called Yangbachen, with less than one hundred families, who trade once a year with Tsurbu in the same produce as the Bangba Bayang people. Many junipers grow here, and the dry wood is taken to Lhasa for firewood. Both the above countries are very much alike and the people dress in Tibetan fashion.

North-west of Yangbachen is Lower Nagtsang, one of the most prosperous of all the nomad countries. Of less area than Golok and Dsachuka, it is larger than Nagchuka, and is mostly grass land, with a few low mountains and many small lakes, which in summer are full of wild duck and cranes. Like the Golok, rich people here live in large tents of yak hair, which are deserted in summer except by the old folk and lamas, the others moving round with the yak. Nagtsang people are very timid; they do not rob, and for that reason plenty of robbers come to them. Two or three robbers with swords and lances can easily intimidate a whole family and drive off their cattle without opposition. The women here wear tiaras of trankas, surmounted by corals, which at night-time they can lift off like a cap. But generally the head-dress, rings, and ear-rings are the same all over the nomad country, except among the Golok and Dsachuka.

West of this country is Upper Nagtsang, equally large and prosperous. Every year the young people of these two countries travel to beyond Shigatse, in Tsang, to sell salt, sheep, and yak, and lay in a store of wheat, barley, and cloth for the coming year. More often the salt is loaded on sheep than on yak, each sheep taking a 5-catty package on either side* ; and, as the caravan may have perhaps 1,000 sheep, to unload which in the evening and re-load in the morning would be too much of a task, the loads are never taken off during the whole journey of twelve to fifteen days. The sheep get into the habit of looking for a stone or some other slight elevation, resting one package on which they so go to sleep.

Bangba Chugdso is a fairly large but poor country of grass lands and snow mountains. Here the people are very poor, so poor that many a family lives in a tent only ten feet square or even less. If one of the family finds himself squeezed out, he makes himself a cave of yak-dung, like the shelters constructed for lambs and calves, and creeps inside. Cheese and butter are not plentiful, as in other nomad countries, and tsamba is very scarce. The Chugdso people live chiefly on meat, eating horse-flesh ; they hunt the wild horse, with guns in summer and with snares in winter. A very strong rope of yak hair, with a heavy stone attached, is lowered through the ice, which soon freezes round it, leaving a loose end on the surface. How they catch the horse with this rope I do not know for certain, for I have not seen it actually done, but I think that it is in the same manner as they snare muskdeer, that is, by a loop at the free end : the wild horse steps in the loop and its efforts to get away only tighten the knot. Muskdeer are always caught in this way, never shot.† Horses' hide is used for making shoes. Wild goats also are hunted for their skins. The religion in Chugdso is mainly Bönbo : there are no lamaseries :

* "Catty" : a Chinese measure = 1⅓ English pounds.

† The trap is described by Rockhill : Notes, p. 714.

hermits live in caves in the mountains. In this country is a big snow mountain called Dargo, northward of which is Lake Dangra.

South of Bangba Chugdso is Yönchödengga, a country not so large as Chugdso but, although its people are nomad, with a village of about twenty houses near a Bön monastery. It is a small trading centre where nomads meet farmers from the south. West of it is a large Geluba lamasery called Darjeling, containing about one hundred lamas.

Then comes a tiny nomad country of twenty to thirty families, called Zhungru, subject not to the Tibetan Government but to the Dalai Lama, who—while other nomads pay taxes to the Debazhung—sends annually a She-Bön, or Cattle Official, to appropriate a certain proportion of the Zhungru cattle, butter, and cheese, all of which are regarded as being the Dalai's property. West of it is the Sachya lamasery, Namjel Lhadse, which the nomads call Dsalung, and the Soda Lake and the Tsala mine. Tsala (Ch. "pai fan") is an article resembling salt or sugar in appearance which is used in amalgamating metals.*

Lower Droshü is a very large nomad country and very prosperous. It has no farms but, what is better, has plenty of wool and salt, so that by trading with Nepal it obtains wheat, barley, red rice, flour, cloth, Indian corn in larger quantities than any other nomad country. The barley is thick-shelled, and for that reason some do not like it for making tsamba, but others prefer it, saying that the taste is superior.

Upper Droshü lies to the north-west. It also is a large country, and the conditions similar to

* Tsala is borax, a Tibetan export.—J. H. E.

those in Lower Droshü. Beyond it is the mountain plateau of Mayum La, from which issues the Horse River, and Mapam Yutso, a lake with eight small lamaseries near it. From here five days north is the village of Barka Dazam, a centre for the distribution of China tea, with a resident magistrate, Dzongbön. South-west of Barka Dazam lies Janyima, and three or four days south-west of that, Jakargo, both wild countries, but the scene every summer of great fairs visited by Indians and Tibetans. The Indians sell sugar-candy, treacle, cloth, sewing-machines, and copper boilers each containing eleven smaller pots inside them. These boilers foreigners call "dickje." The biggest are about eighteen inches in diameter, and are used for boiling tea and rice; they have a lid, but no handles. They sell also a kind of hard wood, which is the goitre-like boss or protuberance that grows on tree trunks. It is in great demand with Tibetans for making tsamba bowls and wine cups, and is very expensive.* The Indians buy salt, burug, sheep, and tea-bricks from China. Burug is a thick woollen cloth, in Chinese "pulo," made in Lhasa; dyed red it is used for cloaks; a thicker variety, striped in eight colours, and sold in rolls of about fifty feet in length by eight inches in width, is used for covering saddles.†

Three to four days north-west of Jakargo is another wild country called Dretaburi.‡ There are

* "Expensive" is of course a relative term. Sherap purchased for me a medium-sized tsamba-bowl of this wood for the equivalent of 8/-.

† Such a roll is sold in Tachienlu for $20, say £2.

‡ Dretaburi: on the Sutlej, the Elephant River.—Sven Hedin, T.-H., III, 207. The lamas in the monastery pronounced the name of the place Tretapuri, but the word Tirtapuri is of Indian origin and signifies "pilgrimage resort."—*Ib.*, p. 196.

no houses there and the nomads are few ; it is chiefly celebrated for its miraculous spring, from which, if you drink, you will not go to purgatory. This is the last of the nomad countries.

CHAPTER X

KAMBA AND LHASAWA.

Kam and Lhasa—Dress: laymen and lamas—Coiffure and Ornaments—Etiquette—Sowing Crops—Harvest—Winter Employment—Tanning—Cattle Fodder—Cattle Slaughter—Cannibalism—Prohibited Flesh—A Tibetan Meal—Preparation of Yak Meat—Yak Blood—Mutton—Recipe for making Tsamba—Butter—Cheese—Tea—Beer and Arag—Use of Tobacco and Snuff.

TIBETANS commonly distinguish themselves as Kamba and Lhasawa, people of eastern and western Tibet respectively. Kam includes all of eastern Tibet, from the Golok country in the north to the Yunnan border in the south, and from Dartsendo in the east to Chamdo in the west. Lhasa, in the broad sense, extends from the nomads in the north to India in the south, and includes Bhutan and Sikhim, but not Nepal; and from Chamdo in the east to and inclusive of Ladak in the west. This is the popular (ethnographical) signification of the terms Kam and Lhasa, and even a Chinese might describe a man from Dartsendo as a Tibetan, although (politically) Dartsendo is no more in Tibet than are Bhutan, Sikhim, and Ladak.

In Kam and Lhasa everyone wears undershirt and trousers, but the principal garment of both men and women is a large gown or cloak (chuba), shaped like a Japanese kimono and made of pulo, or of cloth lined with lamb- or sheep-skin, or of wadded cotton. The colour varies: blue, maroon, and liver colour are the commonest; rarely it is green; sometimes it is of bright stripes. The gown is very roomy and long enough to fall to the ankles, but, caught up by a cloth girdle, it does not reach below the knees (unless worn by a lama), and the left breast is used as a pocket, capacious enough to carry two small babies. The sleeves are half as long again as the arms, and are, perhaps, a foot and a half wide. In Lhasa the gown is a little smaller than in Kam and not caught up so high, and, as worn by Lhasa women, it is sleeveless and covered in front from waist to ankle by a brightly-striped apron.

After the gown, the next most important article of dress is the boot. This comes up to the knee, and in Kam is made of leather, or of cloth with leather upper, and has a sole of yak-skin. The colour of boots varies greatly, but they almost always start with three or four inches of red above the uppers, whether cloth or leather ; round the calf may be perpendicular stripes in blue and yellow and green and white, with crosses ; and above that, up to the knee, the material may be of any colour ; rainbow-coloured silk threads follow the line from the toe-cap to the top of the red. Behind the knee the boot has a slit, and is tied round with a cloth garter of any colour. In Lhasa the boots are more uniform in appearance, being made of blue pulo ; the uppers are always cloth, and the soles are of yak- or goat-hair.

Travelling in Kam men usually carry with them a waterproof cape, made simply of a circular piece of white felt with a round hole in the centre and opening down the front ; women use a white woollen blanket. For head-gear the Kamba wear a Shantung felt cap with ears, or a small red turban. They never walk if they can help it, always travelling on horseback with gun slung on back and sword worn horizontally across the body; usually, too, they carry on the hip a sharp knife about a foot in length. They take great pride in their weapons, horse, and saddle. The Lhasaman does not carry weapons or a felt, nor does he keep a horse.

Lamas' dress differs considerably from that of the ordinary Tibetan. Undergarments are a sleeveless shirt and a skirt of dark red pulo, very wide and reaching to the ankles, tied round the waist by a belt of yellow cloth; also a sleeveless waistcoat of red pulo trimmed with gold thread at the neck and tied by a yellow belt; authority to wear the waistcoat, which is not Buddhist, was granted by Tsongkaba. Outer garments are the maroon gown, which falls to the ankles, and two blankets, one being maroon and worn like a plaid, the other yellow with square patches on it. Gelong are entitled to a second yellow blanket, and wear all three when going to service. Boots are of the common kind, but the uppers are always white, the band round the calf maroon or liver-coloured, and the garters either maroon or yellow. The head is shaved, except in the case of hermits (tsamba). Their caps are high, of a round conical shape, like large peaches. Each sect wears the same shape of cap, but for the Geluba the colour is yellow, for the Nyimaba, Karjuba, and Sachyaba it is red, and for the Bönbo, white. The higher lamas wear caps of various sorts. All carry rosaries, and from the waistbelt depends a square wallet made of cloth, yellow in the case of Geluba, red for the other sects, containing a small brass bottle which they use every morning when washing the mouth, in accordance with Buddha's command.

In Kam men wear the hair short or in a queue; in Lhasa all wear queues. Kam women have their hair dressed in many plaits falling to the waist, each plait ornamented with amber, coral, turquoise, and small floral designs in gold and silver; the crown of the head is decorated with amber ornaments. Lhasa women dress the hair in two thick plaits, one on either side, the ends joined behind the back by a string of pearls if they are wealthy, otherwise of coloured glass, set off with three corals and turquoise; on the head they wear a tiara of red woollen cloth sewn with coral, turquoise, pearls, or coloured glass; in Tsang the two plaits are coiled about the ears, and on the crown is worn a high head-dress of red cloth on a wooden frame, sewn with pearls, coral, and turquoise.

Finger-rings are very popular with both sexes everywhere in Tibet. In Kam men and women wear ear-rings, annular or pendant, but not differentiated. In Lhasa women's ear-rings are larger than men's and are adorned with turquoise, while the men's are adorned with pearl. Necklaces are common everywhere, several being worn, and are made of coral, turquoise, pearls, and other precious stones of various colours. Bracelets of silver and gold are worn in Kam, of white shell in Lhasa.

In the Tibetan home are no chairs or tables, meals are taken off the floor. Men sit cross-legged, but women would be considered immodest if they sat in this fashion; they kneel. In hot weather men may let the gown slip off one shoulder, or both for that matter, but women keep the breast covered.

Food generally is plentiful, and they do not use the Chinese form of salutation : "Have you eaten rice ?" which they regard as a sign of permanent poverty. The greeting in the morning is, "Have you slept well ?" and the equivalent of "Good-night !" is "Sleep well !" In bidding good-bye to a guest the host says "Go slowly !" and the guest replies, "Sit slowly !"—("slowly" having the significance of "sine cura," free from care, in security). When meeting on the road, a social inferior stands aside, holds his hat with both hands against his stomach, puts out his tongue, and bows from the hips. The passer recognises the salutation with a nod. Women salute in the same way, but as they do not wear a hat, merely clasp the hands to the stomach, put out the tongue, and bow. The protrusion of the tongue is a general sign of respect, or awe, or fear. One does it when being told of a person's death, or of a robbery, or other calamity ; when putting out the tongue, the eyes generally protrude at the same time. In interviewing a lama or high official, the Tibetan confines his replies as far as possible to "Yes" and "No," putting out the tongue after each answer. To the lama he kneels, before an official he stands with bowed head and hands clasped to stomach.*

I shall now tell you of the farmers, or yüba. The crops in Kam are wheat, barley, oats (Ti. yu-bo,

* In Tachienlu tribesmen, when putting out the tongue in salutation, hold out one or both hands, palms uppermost, bending the body slightly, eyes also protruding.—(Rockhill ascribes this form of greeting to the Mongols of Tsaidam. —*L. of L.*, p. 146.)

This form of salute is unknown in China in modern times, but it may not always have been so. "This day I have seen Laotzu, and he is like the dragon. At his voice my mouth remained wide open, and I was not able to shut it ; my tongue came out with astonishment, and I have never been able to draw it back again." So spoke Confucius—after paying Laotzu a visit—breaking the silence of three days.—Quoted by Huc, *Christianity in China*, I, 325.

Ch. yen mai), peas, and turnips, the last mainly used after being dried as fodder for cows, goats, and sometimes horses. Towards the end of March the fields are spread with stable-manure and ashes and urine, and the Tsiba is consulted as to an auspicious time for sowing. On the appointed day the sowing is done by the farmer's wife. This is because she is the nor-lha (wealth-idol) of the house ; everything to do with houschold matters and with food is her particular concern. While the farmer attends to the horses and cattle, to buying and selling, the wife is supreme indoors, and it is she who offers tea to visitors. The farmér's wife, then, goes to the field with two bags of seed, a bottle of beer, a da-dar, and a round, shallow basket. She stands the bags upright, unties the mouth, and plants the da-dar in the seed. Next she fills a cup with beer, dips the third finger of her right hand in the liquid, and with her thumb flicks the drop from it towards the sky. This is done three times, being an offering to Buddha, his law, and the priesthood. She also invokes the Zhidag, whom she prays to favour her with an abundant crop and to send no storms. Then she quaffs the cup, waves the da-dar three times (though this part of the ceremony is falling into disuse), and calls on Luck to come. These observances completed, she fills her basket with seed and, supporting it on the left hip, begins to sow.

A man-servant does the ploughing, the plough being pulled by two dso abreast. Should the farmer be very well-to-do, ten or twenty ploughs will be in use at the same time. After the soil has been turned up, one or two women come and rake it smooth.

At the end of June, when the young crop is six

inches out of the ground, everyone goes to look at it. If the soil gets dry, the earth between the stems is carefully broken up with a hoe. The field is never irrigated, as is done in China; in the event of a drought, should appeals to the Nag be in vain, the crop is spoiled.

At this time, too, or in July, the weeds are pulled up; and at the end of September the harvest is gathered, the reaping being done with sickles. Every available animal on the farm is brought into service to carry the sheaves home, where they are stacked on the roof and left to dry. They are then threshed with a flail, which has five or six small sticks loosely tied to its end. After being winnowed on the roof, the grain is taken below and stored in a little room alongside the stable. This done, a holiday is held; a yak is killed and the meat served, with quantities of beer, to all who have taken part in the work. About this time the nomads come down to trade their yak and sheep for grain, the farmer bartering the remains of last year's crop and keeping the new intact. Wheat, barley, oats, and peas are all sown and harvested at the same time; then turnip seed is sown and the crop gathered just before the first frost sets in.

In Lhasa conditions and customs are much the same as in Kam. But in addition to the crops that Kam has, there are mustard, beans, vegetables, a little hemp, and fruit—peaches, apricots, pears, apples, walnuts. The crops are earlier than in Kam, seed being sown in February and harvest gathered at the end of August. The farmer's wife sows from a bag, singing as she sows; the ploughman, too, sings as he ploughs. In fact, although the Kamba are a cheery folk, the Tsangbawa are still more happy, always singing at work, whether it be carrying loads along mountain paths or building a house. The dso that pull the plough have their heads decorated prettily with red wool, and their necks strung with bells. Fields in Lhasa are irrigated and the hoe is not used. Also the grain is not flogged on the roof, but trodden on a threshing-floor by yak and donkeys.

When harvest is over and winter is come the women stay indoors. Before sunrise they are out collecting the still frozen yak-dung for fuel, with which they light the fire and prepare chota-hazri. Their day is spent largely in weaving undyed woollen cloth, nambu (Ch. mu-tzu), and their evenings in carding wool and spinning thread in preparation for the next day's work, by the light of butter-lamps or pine-splinters, dronma shing (Ch. sung kuan). They retire for the night any time after eight o'clock.

Men go out hunting, or cutting timber, or trading. They also make coats and boots, and cure skins. In the latter employment they first of all soak the skin in water and then with a knife scrape off every particle of flesh. This done, the skin is laid in the sun and a mixture of rancid butter and yak- or sheep-brains smeared over it and rubbed in hard by hand. The butter softens the skin and the brains give it whiteness. It is then rolled up, tied round with rope, put out in the sun and rolled with the foot for three or four days, during which it is occasionally opened and stretched by two men pulling on it, until all the water is out of it and it is quite soft and white. Chinese stretch the skins they are tanning on pegs, so as to make them as large as possible, with the result that the hide becomes almost transparent and of low market value.

As regards the feeding of animals, the following is the diet given by well-to-do farmers in Kam; and it obtains in Lhasa also, where, however, there are no yak or dso:—

Yak, dso, and sheep are fed on grass only.

Horses are fed on goat meat, oats, peas, dried turnip, and grass; barley and wheat are not considered sufficiently strengthening.

Lambs are given pea-tsamba, with a pinch of salt in spring-time to make them strong.

Goats, being fewer than sheep, are sometimes given peas, pea-tsamba, and dried turnips.

Cows are fed on grass, peas, turnip leaves, dried turnip, waste tea-leaves, and the barley refuse after making beer; yak prefer wild country to graze in, so nomads have yak and farmers cows.

Pigs, which are few, get peas chiefly, also oats, turnip leaves, dried turnips, refuse barley.

Nomads give their horses goat-meat, butter, and fresh tea-leaves ground up and mixed with salt. They have very few goats, no pigs, and no cows. A bull is kept to breed dso from the yak: it serves the yak of ten to twenty families.

In slaughtering cattle the first object of all Tibetans, who like blood in their meat, is to retain it in the carcase. The commonest method of killing, therefore, is by suffocating. In Kam and Lhasa the animal's mouth and nostrils are tied up tight, and in the course of half an hour or so it expires; but in Lhasa death is hastened by cutting the victim's throat. In the Golok country the yak which is being suffocated is laid on its side with its legs bound, and is beaten with heavy sticks, then turned over and beaten on the other side, the object being to ensure a good mixture of blood in the meat and fat. In western nomad countries—Nagchuka, Chugdso, the Dise district—the animal is placed on its back, a slit made down the belly, and an artery extracted, called the Artery of Life (sok-tsa or tse-tsa), the slaughterer being careful that all the blood falls back into the carcase. Western nomads also kill by a stab to the heart ; in the case of yak the knife is inserted between the shoulder and the neck, in front ; in that of sheep, a skewer is thrust in below the shoulder blade.

Creatures that the lama law forbids man to eat are, besides man himself, the horse, the cow, and the pig. The prohibition against cannibalism is natural, and the practice does not exist in Tibet, except in the single instance of the Jöba lama when offering corpses to the eagles. Tibetans like to tell a story that in making the hard pilgrimage, lasting one month, round Tsa-Ri in the Ne-Ri, near Bomi, where Dorje Pamo lives, sick pilgrims left behind on the road are driven to eat their dead comrades, because the aborigines, Lo-Ba (Abors), will neither sell nor buy anything. But that, if true, is very exceptional.*

As for horse, cow, and pig flesh, the inhibition is due to the facts that Tamdin, the Chöjong of the Geluba, has a horse's head and neck ;† the Jig-je,

* Waddell (*Lamaism*, p. 518) has a note to the effect that in preparing the thigh-bone trumpet it is the common practice to eat a portion of the human skin covering the thigh-bone. Sherap will not hear of it ; human skin is sometimes used for this purpose but it is never eaten. But eating the ling-ga in the devil dance is a relic of cannibalism.

† Surmounting his other heads.

yidam of the Geluba, has a bull's head; and Dorje Pamo has a growth of pig's bristles behind the ear, or, according to another story, an excrescence there resembling a pig's head. So the eating of those creatures would offend these deities. Buddha's law particularly forbids the eating of pigs, fish, and eggs, but these are not avoided for that reason, Buddha's commands usually being disregarded, but because they are regarded as unclean. Fish are classed among insects and reptiles, like snakes and frogs. In places like Lhasa and Dartsendo, where foreign ways are copied, both pork and fish are eaten; and nomads are sometimes obliged to eat horse-flesh.

In any case, chicken and eggs would not go very far in satisfying a Tibetan appetite. At a single meal he consumes one or two catties of meat, half a catty of tsamba, at least two ounces of butter, seven or eight bowls of tea, and may finish off with a bowl of cold milk curd. He never suffers from indigestion, but tapeworm is universal and the cause of many deaths. Muscularly one Tibetan is the equal of two Chinese; he can also endure cold remarkably, frequently going in a snowstorm with the right shoulder bare.

The meat most commonly eaten is yak. Yaks are slaughtered in the autumn, when they have got fat after pasturage. First the liver, stomach, and intestines are taken out and then the carcase is cut into five large pieces, namely the shoulders, haunches, and breast. The liver is hung up to freeze, and next morning is cut up and eaten raw, though occasionally it is cooked. If several animals have been killed, the surplus of sausages is put inside a stomach and hung up outside the tent for a night to freeze; first thing next morning they are taken down and buried in yak-dung until required, the sides of the dung-heap being built sufficiently steep to prevent dogs from climbing up and scavenging. The five large pieces are frozen, wrapped in yak-skin, and buried in the same manner. Meat required for journeys is cut in long thin strips and hung up for perhaps a week; frozen by night and unfrozen by day, it is gradually dried and then stowed away in bags in the tent for future use. These are the customs in the nomad countries, where meat is eaten raw or cooked in about equal proportions. In Kam it is usually eaten raw and, as it does not always freeze properly it is often tainted, but the Kamba prefer it a little "high." In Lhasa cooked meat is preferred, and not much sausage is eaten. On the other hand the Lhasawa show greater variety in the preparation of dishes than is the case in other parts of Tibet, and they are fond of meat soup, meat balls, and meat chopped up and mixed with rice or with flour.

In Kam and nomad countries, when the yak is shorn in May or June, it is customary to tap certain blood-vessels in its neck with the object of making it stronger. When this is being done the yak is given a lump of butter. The blood is put in plates, sprinkled with salt, and allowed to curdle, after which it is boiled and the water poured off. It then presents an appearance like cooked liver, and is cut in slices and eaten with butter.

The sheep is cut in four pieces, shoulders and haunches, and in Kam and nomad countries is prepared for eating in the same way as yak meat. In Lhasa it is occasionally cooked and eaten at once.

More often it is dried, not in strips but in whole pieces. In Lhasa one sometimes sees dried mutton which is five years old, shrunk very much in size of course. According to a very old Tibetan custom a leg of mutton is kept for an important guest and placed before him at the feast. But he is not intended to eat it; if in ignorance he does so, it is a great breach of etiquette. This dish is known as the der-den, or plate-meat, and serves as a plate for the real course, fresh beef or mutton being placed on top of it. Special delicacies in Lhasa are raw, frozen liver, which is cut and eaten with tsamba; sheep's lungs, stuffed with cooked rice, butter, and spices, hung up to dry, and cooked when required; sheep's head, a special dainty (the host is doing very well if he serves sheep's head on the der-den), and jelly from sheep's trotters, mixed with tsamba.

Tsamba is the staple article of diet. Take some barley, wash it, and put it in boiling water for five minutes. Strain off the water, put the barley in a bag, and keep it overnight in a warm place. In the morning fry it in a pan, stirring round with a stick to prevent it burning. Empty the pan into a bag of cloth or leather, lay the bag on the floor, and roll it backwards and forwards with your feet. Take out and spread in a windy place, so that the chaff is blown away. Then grind in the water-mill, and the resulting meal is tsamba. Nomads use a hand-mill.* A method of frying sometimes used in Kam and Lhasa is to put some fine sand in a clay pot and heat till the sand is red hot; then pour the tsamba on top, shake round, and strain the sand through an iron sieve.

* Quern.

Tsamba is not eaten dry. You fill a tsamba bowl about one-fifth full of tea and put in the tsamba with a good lump of butter and some "dry cheese." Mix it all by kneading with fingers, and eat from hand. Tibetans eat as much butter at one meal as foreigners in two days. "Pea-tsamba" is made from peas instead of barley ; it is eaten by the poorer people and by servants.

The usual Tibetan way of making butter is by sinking the pail in the ground and churning, the churner relieving the monotony of the process by singing "one-two-three," "one-two-three." In nomad countries they have a different method. The nomad woman takes a yak-skin bag of, say, 40-catty capacity, fills it half full of milk, and adds a little sour milk, perhaps two catties. She then blows into the bag and, having filled the empty half with air, ties it at the neck and, kneeling down, rolls it backwards and forwards on the ground with her hands for one or two hours. At first the sound is that of a liquid, then of something thicker, and finally of liquid again, indicating to the woman that the milk and butter are separated. She pours the contents into a pail, to which she adds a little water, cold in summer, warm in winter. Having washed her hands, she lifts out the butter which has risen to the top, kneads it, makes it into a ball, and drops it into cold water. In spring the butter is white, in autumn and winter yellow. This is due to the fact that in spring there is little grass, and what there is is very dry, and there is no fat on the animals. They get stronger as the summer advances, and by autumn are fat.

The milk left after the butter has been lifted out of the pail is boiled, and cheese forms at the bottom of the pot. It is not very good, but it is dried, crumbled into grains, and commonly used to mix with tsamba. Nomads like this "dry cheese" because it keeps a long time, two or three years. A better cheese is made as follows. Boil your milk, pour off into pail, add a little sour milk, cover with cloth, and stand it in a warm place for twelve hours. In the evening pour the curds into a thin cotton bag and hang up for twenty-four hours to let the water drop out. The cheese so formed is white in colour and very good. Another kind of cheese, which some prefer to the last, is made by boiling the milk, adding a little sour milk, and boiling again until the milk gets thin and you see cheese formed at the bottom. This kind of cheese is kneaded in the hand and becomes like india-rubber, so that you can pull it out long, tie knots in it, or make it into a ball. Again, clean the pail thoroughly to start with and put milk into it for six months without recleaning. At the end of the half-year you have an excellent cheese an inch thick on the inside of the pail.

Tea in nomad countries is drunk with milk in it. The Kamba on the other hand drink "black tea." A piece is broken off the brick and put in a pot of cold water on the stove. A little soda is added to draw out the colour. When it has boiled for some time, more cold water is added and it is boiled again, altogether for two hours. It is then taken out and strained and some salt put in. Most other Tibetans, and all lamas, wherever they may be, drink "butter tea." After the tea is boiled, butter and salt are added and the mixture is churned until it resembles tea with milk in it. Butter tea is not much favoured in Kam, except at Daṛtsendo, where they sometimes add pounded walnuts to the mixture. At Gyangtse, Tibetan and foreign customs are blended in the concoction of Indian tea, with butter, salt, and an egg in it, to which are added milk and sugar, the whole being churned into butter tea.

Apart from tea, the only other beverages in Tibet that require preparation are beer and arag, and of these the Tibetans drink great quantities, the women as much as the men. Beer (chang) is the general drink, but in Kam arag is very popular with both sexes. Nomads do not have either. Buddhism of course regards wine as one of the chief causes of sin. The story is told of a very good disciple of Buddha that once, travelling through a village, he was invited by a woman to kill her goat for her, drink her wine, and sleep with her. In spite of his repeated refusals she persisted and would not let him go. At last he thought to get off by complying with the least sinful of the three requests and drank the wine she pressed on him. Unfortunately he got drunk, lay with her, and killed her goat.

Both beer and arag are made from barley (ne). After washing your barley carefully, put it in water on the stove to boil, and do not take it off until all the water is boiled away. Then remove the barley and spread it out to cool on bamboo mats—these are procured from Nepal, Bhutan, and Sikhim—or on a clean blanket. Add a little tsamba and some yeast (Ti. pab ; Ch. chü-tzu) and mix well. Now put the boiled barley, or "lum" as it is called, in a large pot with a narrow neck and a bunghole at its base, and place near stove with heavy cloth over it. Leave for three days and three nights. If after that period it smells right, neither sweet nor sour, remove the spigot and tap the beer. Thirty catties of barley should produce about five catties of this first brew, which is the best; you keep it for yourself and do not give it to friends. Fill up the pot again with water, warm or cold according as you prefer the brew to be a little sour or a little sweet. The pot can be filled up three times, but of course the brew gets weaker each time, and sourer and more windy on the stomach. The refuse barley from the pot is given to cows and pigs; yak will not eat it.

To make arag, remove the barley after the first brew and place in large vessel with two ears. From string passed through the ears suspend a small pot inside, in such a way that it does not touch the barley. Place a tightly-fitting pan of iron or clay over the mouth of the vessel and fill it with ice, or with cold water if ice is not procurable. Put the vessel on a hot fire and keep the pan supplied with ice. The steam from the barley condenses on the cold lid and is distilled into the small pot in the form of arag. You will get perhaps two catties of arag at the first brew and you can make a second and a third brew from the same barley, but weaker.

Tobacco (tama) is in common use both for smoking and as snuff. It is obtained from China, and from Nepal, Bhutan, and Sikhim. The leaves of the rhubarb plant, known in Lhasa as "cho-lo" (Ch. suan chiang), are also used for smoking. The Tibetan woman does not smoke; if she did, she would be laughed at and called Chinese; but she takes snuff. About seventy per cent. of men and women are snuff-takers; this figure includes nomads and lamas, who do not smoke.

CHAPTER XI

CONTACT WITH CHINESE : TRADE.

Chuko Liang's long bow—The stratagem of the sheep—The Kings of Mi-nyag and Chala—The Aja—Duke Yo in Jyade and Nangchen—Norbu Zangbö—Modern Trade Customs—The Tea Trade—Caravans—Routes across Tibet.

MANY years ago, when Tibetan territory extended eastward so as to include Kiungchow and Kiating,* a famous Chinese general called K'ung Ming† warred against the savage tribes, who were comprehensively called Mantze, but were really Miao, living on the border of Yunnan and Tibet towards Kueichow ; their king was one Chijen Monghu. The war was a very bitter one and lasted for a long time,‡ but at length K'ung Ming prevailed and came up north for further conquests. At Kiungchow he found many other Mantze, really Böd people, who were

* Cities of Szechuan, west and south of Chêngtu respectively.

† K'ung Ming is the literary style of Chuko Liang, A.D. 181–234, a native of Shantung and one of China's most popular military heroes.—See Giles, *Biog. Dict.*, Art. 459.

‡ According to Chinese legend Mêng Hu, when captured by Chuko Liang, refused to admit the superiority of the Chinese general, whereupon the latter released him, telling him to try again. This happened seven times, after which Mêng Hu cried "pax," acknowledged his inferiority, and submitted to Chinese rule. When censured by the emperor for his leniency, Chuko explained that it would have been impossible to hold these remote and mountainous regions by force, and that their submission depended entirely on their conviction of Chinese superiority. The scene of the campaign is said to have been Chien Ch'ang Valley, which thereafter remained peacefully subject to the Chinese, at least during Chuko's life-time.

then living in barbarous conditions*; in fact they were the same people as inhabited the caves near Kiating, known among Chinese to this day as "Caves of the Mantze" (Man Tung).† Well, after some hard fighting K'ung Ming drove them out of the Kiungchow district. Wishing to bring the long campaign to a satisfactory end, and being a very resourceful general, he offered peace on the terms that the Böd people should cede to him whatever tract of land could be covered by a shot from his bow. They agreed. K'ung Ming then bent his bow, and that so strongly, that the arrow flew far to the west and out of sight of the onlookers. Eventually, after much searching, it was found on Dsamdrag, the mountain overlooking Dartsendo on the north,‡ where K'ung Ming's emissaries had secretly planted it; and believing that K'ung Ming must be a very powerful spirit, the Tibetans stood by their terms and ceded to China all the country up to Dsamdrag.§

* Tibetans, from whatever part of the country they come, speak of themselves as Böd-pa (Böd people). The word "Tibet" represents two Tibetan words meaning "Upper Böd," by which name the central and western portions of Tibet are occasionally called by the natives, to distinguish them from the eastern portion, which is sometimes referred to as Man Böd, meaning "Lower Böd." Mongols speak of Tibet as Tangut.—Rock., *Notes on Ethnology of Tibet.*

Tibet proper, that is the provinces of Tsang and U, are known to the people as Pö (pronounced like the French word *peu*).—*Bell*, p. 12.

One of the Chinese names for Tibet is T'u-fan, the old sound of *fan* being *po*.—Giles, *Dict.*

"Mantze" was a term used by Marco Polo, applied by him to all tribes living south of the Yangtse.

† For a generation a controversy has been going on, of the usual acrimonious kind to which sinologues have accustomed us, as to whether these caves were ever inhabited or whether they were not merely used as tombs.

‡ About 100 miles as the crow flies.

§ The Chinese occupation of Tachienlu was not made effective until the early 18th century, when the famous Yo Chung-ch'i established a garrison there. Rockhill says: "Prior to 1700 Tachienlu and the country east of it, for nearly 100 miles, was not occupied by the Chinese and was under the rule of the King of Chala, but since that date this tract has been annexed to China, though the natives have been allowed to retain their tribal organization."—*L. of L.*, p. 276.

Here in those days were no houses of course, and when K'ung Ming came to inspect the area covered by his arrow's flight, he, being cautious, approached the place not by the direct Luting road, but round by Mosimien. Even so he found the surrounding hills all held by Tibetans, prepared to offer a formidable resistance to the small force which commissariat difficulties would allow him to bring up.

But to one of K'ung Ming's bold and ingenious turn of mind the problem was an easy one. He solved the commissariat difficulty by feeding his troops on mutton, taking with him large droves of sheep for the purpose; and he concealed the smallness of his force by marching only at night and tying a lantern on each sheep. When the Tibetans saw this apparently immense army moving on them in the darkness, they broke and fled, and K'ung Ming camped on what is now Dartsendo.*

All this country of Chala was then included in Mi-nyag, a name now reserved to the country three days out on the south road. Now there was a king in Mi-nyag who, while out hunting one day, wounded a deer on the top of the Jedo Pass and pursued it in this direction. After a long and tiring chase he gave up the pursuit, finding himself in the pleasant valley where K'ung Ming was encamped. The

* Another famous instance of Chuko Liang's ingenuity is recorded in the story of the arrows: In Szechuan's war against the formidable Ts'ao Ts'ao (whose name lives in the proverb: "Talk of Ts'ao Ts'ao and he will appear") he was ordered by the jealous generalissimo, Chou Yü, to provide 100,000 arrows within ten days or lose his head. The task seemed impossible, but Chuko replied boldly that, in order to avert defeat, he must get the arrows within three days. With 20 junks, each laden with 1,000 sheaves of straw "ranged like leaves" and covered with cloth, he dropped down the Yangtse by night in a surprise attack on Ts'ao Ts'ao. The latter's troops in panic shot all their arrows into the dim floating shapes and, when the straw was full of them, Chuko returned to Chou Yü with the required number. Ts'ao Ts'ao, being depleted of his stock, was left open to the attack next day.—N.C.B.R.A.S., vol. liv, p. 3.

latter gave him hearty welcome, allowed him to build a house (the remains of which, behind the Catholic Mission, are still called "The Old Yamen"), and recognised him as headman of the district. By the time of the Manchus this king's family had all died out, with the exception of one old lady and her grandsons; and the Manchus erected the State of Chala and made the old lady Queen of Chala. In due course her grandson became king, and the line was carried on until 1922 when the then King of Chala, who had been arrested and put in prison by the Chinese, met his end in an attempt to escape, his body being found at the river side. Two sons by secondary wives are still alive here in Dartsendo, and in accordance with Tibetan custom they are regarded as rightful heirs.*

When K'ung Ming returned to China he left behind him forty-eight soldiers, who married native women and settled permanently. Hence the place was known as the Settlement of the forty-eight families—in Chinese Ssushihpa Chia Gochuang, in Tibetan, Aja-Kaba Zhi-ju-zhe-je. "Aja" is not a Tibetan word, and is used only in Dartsendo; it may be Mantze or Jyarong dialect. It is equivalent to the Tibetan "Kalon" or "Lhunbo." It denotes an official lower than a king but higher than a Bön, headman. Thus we have in Chala the grades King, Aja, Headman. The Aja are like the Kaji in Sikhim, the Maharajah's ministers. The descendants of the

* The "Record of the Establishment of the Province of Western Kam," published at Chêngtu in 1912 by the ex-Warden of the Marches, Fu Sung-mu, states that the country round Tachienlu was originally known as Mao Niu Kuo, but in the time of the Mings, for its friendliness to China, the name was changed to Ming Chêng. Ming Chêng, or to give it its Tibetan name, Chala, was incorporated in the province of Szechuan in 1904, and was called K'ang T'ing Prefecture.

forty-eight families are still called Aja by the Tibetans in Dartsendo.*

Another Chinese general famous in Tibetan annals, though quite modern compared with Chuko Liang, was Jador Abar, who conquered Jyade and Nangchen.† Sönam Yungdrung, who is a native of Jyade, or Sanshihchiu Ts'u as the Chinese call it (the Tibetan word meaning "Chinese people," and the Chinese "The 39 Clans"), and prefers China to Jyade, though unable to talk Chinese, tells me that in the old days his country was called Chumbo, and was divided into two parts, Black and White Chumbo, each being under a Tussu or Chief. It was conquered by a Mongol king from Gurzhu, called Dendsin Chöjel, to whom thereafter the inhabitants paid annual tribute in horses. But Dendsin was attacked by Jador Abar, who was sent by the Manchu Emperor, and who was ambitious to conquer all Tibet. The general came from Szechuan, although that may not have been his native province, bringing with him only thirty-eight soldiers, but, with military help from Kansu, he succeeded in driving out Dendsin, who retired to Mongolia. Jador Abar then divided the country into thirty-nine chieftaincies, one under each of his soldiers and one under himself; and each chief paid to the Chinese amban an annual tax of Tls.450 in silver. That is how the country came

* Sherap's account of the origin of the Aja is the traditional one. Rockhill says that the hereditary chiefs of the eighteen states into which Eastern Tibet is divided appoint a certain number of civil and military officers to assist them in the government of the country, a large proportion of them being taken from among the Ku-ts'a or bodyguard, whose charges are hereditary. These officers receive no pay, but each has a grant of land in perpetuity, and they have frequently the exclusive privilege of lodging high officials and caravans passing through their towns, a source of considerable profit. In Chala the Ku-ts'a are known as Agia and there are 58 (*sic*).—*L. of L.*, p. 218.

† Jador Abar is Yo Chung-ch'i, Duke Yo.

to be called by the Chinese "The Thirty-nine Clans." The Secretary says that this account is not taken from books, but has been handed down by tradition. He adds that, since the Revolution (1911), the Tibetans have recovered the country; the thirty-nine chiefs have no longer any power, but pay to the Debazhung through two Dzongbön the same taxes as everyone else.

He also states that the country called Erhshihwu Ts'u ("The 25 Clans"), adjoining Jyade on the north, which still preserves its old Tibetan name of Nangchen, used to be independent, like Derge. It was at that time divided into twenty-five districts, each under a Bön and all under a Jelbo or King, but it was conquered by Jador Abar and handed over to the Kansu people as a reward for their assistance. Kansu permitted the Jelbo to retain his throne, but exacted an annual tax in silver, paid to the Kansu official at Jyekundo.*

Trade at Dartsendo began with the arrival of Norbu Zangbö ("Good Jewel"), the first Tibetan to become a merchant. It is said that he was a native of Samye, had travelled all over Tibet, and at last reached Dartsendo, but as to his route tradition is silent. After seeing conditions here, he returned to Lhasa and came back with a caravan of musk,

* These stories are recorded for what they may be worth: at anyrate they reflect popular beliefs. They refer to the troublous period in the first half of the eighteenth century, when the Chinese were threatened by a combination of Tibetans with the Oelöt tribes of Ili, over the identity of the seventh Dalai Lama. The Chinese were obliged to acquiesce in the Tibetan choice, although Yo Chung-chi's expedition against Tibet met with little difficulty. That was in 1720. Subsequently, in 1732, when the tribes south of Koko Nor were reorganised, 39 clans, comprehending 4,889 families, were placed under the jurisdiction of the Sining amban, to whom they paid an annual tax of Tls. 391.12, or at the rate of Tls. .08 per family. In 1908, three years before the revolution, Chao Erh-fêng diverted this payment from the amban to the Chinese Government.

deer-horns, and skins; he brought no wool, as at that time the Chinese did not know how to weave it. For these commodities he received in exchange silk, tea, porcelain, tobacco, and other China produce. His caravan animals were all mules or dso, as the yak is not of much use on a long journey. Although there were no robbers then in Tibet, his servants, whom legend puts at 500 in number, were armed with bows. Trade was done by barter, because in those days Tibet did not have much silver.

I may mention that subsequently wool was brought from Dsachuka, Adra Dsamar, and other nomad countries; and, when factories started in Shanghai, it developed into a very big trade; during the last three or four years it has greatly fallen off.

This pioneer's name is still used in common talk as a synonym for a merchant prince; and a couplet from a popular song runs:—

Dzongbön Norbu Zangbö
Ja Ja Böd la drang kën,

celebrating the fact that it was he who introduced China tea to Tibet.* His headquarters in this district were at a place in the Mi-nyag country called Dorra Garmo, three days out along the south road. About half a *li* off the road white stones can still be seen which marked the site of his compound, but there are no houses there now, only a nomad's tent sometimes in summer; it is all grass-land.

Norbu Zangbö was followed by many other traders, who in course of time brought with them much silver and gold which they obtained from India. Up to three or four years ago, before trade

* Rockhill mentions that tea was introduced into Tibet from China in the reign of Songdsengombo's grandson (Notes, p. 672). This would be about the end of the seventh century of our era.

began to fall off, a single merchant might bring as much as thirty to forty mule-loads of silver and one or two loads of gold, each load being 650 ounces.

Nowadays, when Tibetans make purchases from Chinese merchants, the practice is for them to pay one-half of the purchase price down and to promise the rest when they come back next trip. This way of trading would seem to indicate that the Chinese merchant is very trustful, but as a matter of fact he is well covered. In the first place the Tibetan almost invariably keeps his word; he could not continue in the business if he did not. And in the second, the merchant sells at rather over double what it has cost him to lay the goods down in Dartsendo. For example, he will charge Tls. 1,000 for what has cost him, freight and everything included, Tls. 400; and he receives Tls. 500 down and promise of another Tls. 500 later on. As his business is extensive, embracing perhaps a dozen different buyers, even if two of these were to let him down, a very unlikely event, his profit would still be satisfactory.

With old-established firms, as with friends, business is put through without paper. The use of paper, the "p'iao" system, is quite new, introduced from China. A common procedure is as follows: A, a Tibetan with a consignment of skins but without money to purchase the tea he wants to take back, trades his skins to B, who has no money to pay him. A then buys his tea from the merchant C, by an I.O.U., which B promises C that he will honour in due course. B does not endorse the note, but merely gives his word; this is sufficient, for his reputation would be irretrievably ruined if he played any tricks.

At present Tibetans are not bringing in much silver; they do not seem to be able to get it from India. The Chinese here dislike Tibetans; it is not as in Kansu, where the natives are very similar to Tibetans. Moreover, the civil war in Szechuan has made all Chinese commodities so dear, and local officials are so insatiable in their demands for money, that the Tibet-China trade is now being diverted from Dartsendo to Sining in Kansu, for Peking and Tientsin. Lhasa trades almost entirely with India.

The staple trade is tea. It is brought from China in the form of bricks wrapped in basket-work packages and carried by coolies on the back, the usual load being nine packages of seventeen catties each.* From Dartsendo the tea is distributed over Tibet in two ways. In the "small road business" (hsiao lu) it is carried by yak to Litang and Jyekundo and places on this side of these towns, the tea being left in the original packages but wrapped loosely in yak-skin. In this business the tea-brick is usually of very inferior quality. In the "big road business" (ta lu) the tea goes by yak caravan to Lhasa, the loads not being broken this side of Jyekundo. At Dartsendo the cost of a tea-brick such as is used in the Lhasa trade averages, for good and indifferent qualities, about Rs. 1½; purchasing in large quantities for export it would work out at an average of R.1.†

* One carrier whom I passed on the road had on his back sixteen packages of eighteen catties each, = 374½ lbs., but he was not travelling more than about seven miles a day. I am assured that, for such short distances, 28 stone is no uncommon weight, and that heavier loads are known.

† Money Table :—

5 Karma (cents)	=	1 Pice.
6 Pice	=	1 Tranka, about 3d.
3 Trankas	=	1 Chinese Rupee, about 9½d.
2½ Rupees	=	Mex. $1.

Tea for Lhasa is taken out of its original packages and sewn into yak-skin, twelve bricks of three catties each being sewn in one skin cover. This makes half a load. The charge for repacking it is Rs. 4½ per load of seventy-two catties. The load is just the same for mules as for yaks, and is small because of the length of the journey. Carriage is by stages—to Dawu, Kanze or Rongbatsa, Dsogchen, Jyekundo, Nagchuka or Damba, Lhasa. Half the freight is paid at the beginning of each stage and half at the end. The freight, which is fairly regular in amount, is based on the estimated normal length of the stage. For example, from Dartsendo to Dawu is seven days, and the freight varies between Rs. 3 and Rs. 5 per load, according to the quantity of tea in the market and the number of animals available. But yaks, fond of grazing by the road, and usually reluctant to travel in the afternoon, may take one or two months to do the stage, and yet the freight charge remains the same.

As a rule the owner of the tea does not himself accompany it ; he leaves the business in the hands of an agent, who goes ahead and makes all arrangements at the different stages. At the first stage, Dawu, he meets yak-owners from Kanze or Rongbatsa, strikes a bargain for carriage to that town, waits for the caravan to arrive, pays off the balance due on the first stage, and goes ahead again. For these services he gets no salary, but his food is paid, and the merchant lends him a horse, saddle, gun, and Tls. 300–400 to do business on his own account. The merchant generally follows behind with a mule caravan of more valuable China produce, such as silks, etc.

Freight from Dartsendo to Rongbatsa averages Rs. 9.75 per load, from there to Jyekundo, Rs. 8; and thence to Lhasa, Rs. 15; a total of Rs. 32.75 on the top of the original price of Rs. 24. Godown rent is one brick per 100 loads for any length of time. At Dsogchen is levied a Government military tax of one brick per eight loads, and at Lhasa a tax of twelve bricks on every ten loads. The tea handed to the Debazhung at Lhasa is meant for the three lamaseries of Serra, Drebung, and Galden, in lieu of the subsidy which, previous to the 1911 Revolution, they used to get from the Peking Government. A merchant estimates that, if he starts out with 1,500 loads, after paying all charges, such as packing, freight, godown rent, taxes, agent's food, etc., he is left with 1,000 loads to sell in Lhasa. For these he gets about Rs. 6 per brick; a few years ago the price was Rs. 8 or 10, but it has been going down of late. Cheap tea is the more profitable because of the larger market. The caravan takes a year to reach Lhasa and allowances must be made for losses on the road and deterioration; also it may arrive at a bad time, with a fully stocked market, and no offers even at Rs. 6. But generally speaking there is a very fair margin of profit.

At Dartsendo, after the tea caravan has left, the merchant continues his preparations for a mule caravan, carrying silks, etc., which he will himself take to Lhasa, not employing agents. The caravan consists of anything from 30 to 100 mules, and with it are some twenty well-armed servants on horseback. The merchant takes several tents, and does the journey quietly at the rate of about fifty *li* per day, stopping when the surroundings are attractive, and perhaps doing a little shooting. There is no need for hurry. He sets out four or five months after the tea, but, following the same road, his mules can do the trip easily in three months. He does not take much money with him, as by bartering some of his goods he can get any extra food required and fresh meat on the road ; and for his mules and horses, grass and peas can be purchased for a handful of tea, a small quantity of which he carries for the purpose. He arrives at Lhasa two or three months ahead of his tea caravan and, while waiting for it, disposes of his merchandise for silver or gold—silver not being very popular, as trankas are not used in Kam ; or he exchanges them for burug or for other Lhasa or India goods.

The stages described follow the route generally known as the Merchants' Road to Lhasa. It goes rather far north but, by doing so, avoids the difficult mountainous country.

Besides the Merchants' Road there are two others between Kam and Lhasa : (1) the Chinese official road, along which the ambans from Peking used to pass ; from Dartsendo it follows what is called the South Road (nan lu), as opposed to the North Road via Kanze (pei lu), and goes due west to Litang and Batang and on through Jamda. It traverses a poor country, without grass or trees, and crosses several very high mountains, but the journey can be done in sixty ordinary stages. It is hardly used now, and for some years the section between Litang and Batang has been almost impassable owing to the activity of the Hsiangchengwa and other brigand tribes. (2) Between the Merchants' and the Official Roads, starting from Kanze, is a road followed by pilgrims ; the high mountains encountered on this route deter traders, but the country is warm and there is much farm land and forests. It is of about the same length as the northern route and is followed by pilgrims because, being remote from trade centres, food is very plentiful and cheap. This road goes from Kanze through the middle of Derge by Lhoko to Riwoche—Chungbo—Nagshe—Gongbo—Dagbo—Lhasa.*

* For details of routes see Appendix II.

CHAPTER XII

ANCHORITES.

The Seeker after Knowledge—The Doer of Good Works—Aspirants to Power: (1) The Chöjong Hermit—The Agba—(2) The Dsalungba.

THERE are five kinds of hermit: the book hermit, whose object in secluding himself is to attain knowledge; the "good-works" hermit, who aspires to reach Dewajen by diligence in good works, and who may be either (1) lama or (2) layman; the chöjong hermit and the dsalungba, both of whom aim at acquiring peculiar powers.

The book hermit is a lama who shuts himself in a cave in the mountains or in a cell in the lamasery for a term of nine years, nine months, and nine days for the purpose of prayer and study. He may engage in conversation twice a day for about an hour at a time, once in the morning and once in the evening, but he does not show himself. His visitors are friends and relatives or, if he is wealthy, business men who seek instructions about his property. When he is prepared to talk he rings a bell. He has generally two meals a day, but sometimes only one; and, before eating, he washes his hands and offers a little tsamba in the form of dorma to the Yidag or Hungry Spirits, whom he calls by sounding his ding-hsiak.* When he has completed his exact

* These resemble miniature cymbals, but they are not struck in the same way; the rim of one is rung against the rim of the other. The only other occasion on which this particular instrument is used is when tsamba is burned in the death-chamber.

term of years, months, and days, he comes out and thereafter enjoys great repute as a lama of much knowledge and one whom the gods are likely to favour.

The good-works hermit relies on deeds rather than knowledge and remains a hermit until he dies. Good works are manifested through six different agencies, namely: through the Eyes, by regarding chöjong, lamas, holy mountains—through the Ears by listening to lamas' talk and to the scriptures—through the Mouth, by reciting scriptures, by praying, and by good talk—through the Body, by fasting and making prostrations—through the Hands, by turning prayer-wheels and making prayer-flags—and through the Feet, by circumambulating holy mountains and making pilgrimages to holy places. But it is the mind that matters. If the mind is bad, it is like a lake of poison; if the eyes are bad, they are like pools of blood; if the mouth is bad, it is like flames of fire; if the hands are bad, they are like swords; and if the feet are bad, they are like lightning, that is to say, as deadly to man's soul as his feet are to innumerable insects.

The good-works hermit rises three hours after midnight, rings a bell and rattles a damaru, to let the gods know that he is about to pray. All the day is occupied in reading prayer-books, praying, and doing good works through the six different agencies; and he has only one meal daily, at midday. His method of praying in the evening is as follows: facing the west, where Obame lives, he stands with palms together, supposedly enclosing a jewel, and touches successively first his forehead, then his lips, then his breast. In touching the forehead he invokes the body of Buddha, who resides in the crown of the head. In touching the mouth, he invokes Buddha's law. And in touching the breast, he invokes Buddha's mind.* He then kneels down with palms flat on the ground and makes a single kotow. These two performances are repeated one after the other many hundred times; if the lama's physique is very strong, he may repeat them a thousand times. Each day is the same until he dies: he may live thus for thirty years.

When a man gets a little old, he begins to think of his past sins and to be afraid of going to Hell. So a layman may decide to leave his wife and family and all earthly concerns and devote the remainder of his life to good works. His first procedure is to have his hair shorn, all save one lock; then he goes to a good lama, who severs that single lock just as the abbot does to the pupil of sixteen entering on his noviciate. Returning home, he then discards his layman's dress and assumes one of a yellow or maroon colour, but of a different cut from a lama's. He no longer cohabits with his wife, or engages in worldly affairs, but spends all his time praying and reading prayer-books and looking for a cave to retire to. In front of the cave he builds a little shack, in which a servant boy of fifteen or so lives and attends to his few wants. He teaches scripture to the boy, who has liberty to go out and in as he pleases, and he talks to visitors twice a day. He has two meals daily, brought to him by his wife or

* Waddell says: "The lama gently touches his forehead, either with the finger or with the bell, uttering the mystic OM, then he touches the top of his chest, uttering AH, then the epigastrium, uttering HUM. It is alleged that the object of these manipulations is to concentrate the parts of the Sattva, namely the body, speech, and mind, upon the image or divinity which he is about to communicate with.—*Lamaism*, p. 423.

children, and he makes tea for himself whenever he wants it. If the cave is not to his liking, he moves to another. And so he lives until he dies.

The Chöjong lama spends his time cultivating the chöjong by beating big drums, ringing bells, rattling the damaru, clashing cymbals, and offering chöba with dorma and brass bowls of tea and wine, telling his beads and repeating the short formula of prayer appropriate to the chöjong. He occupies a small cell in the lamasery and sees no one. Thus he lives for anything from one to seven years, waiting for a chöjong to appear to him. When, say, the Jig-je appears, his term as hermit is finished, and he comes out with the firm conviction that he is henceforth sure of the Jig-Je's help and that of chöjong generally. He is, of course, much in request by persons desiring the chöjong's assistance.

In this connection I may tell you of Arig Rajel Gomba in the Golok country, a monastery which I think is not mentioned in any book: Pedma Rinchen told me about it. Its name is Rongbo Regong, and it houses 1,900 monks of the Dsogchen sub-sect of the Nyimaba. These are not ordinary lamas, because their rules permit them to eat meat, to drink wine, to marry, and to wear the hair long, all contrary to Buddhist law, whatever may be the individual lama's practice, and, though they wear a lama's gown, it is of a white colour. They are known as Agba, and have a great name as sorcerers and exorcisers of devils. On initiation the aspirant is given a cell, and his object is to remain in the cell until he has seen the Za, one of the most powerful and most dreaded chöjong in Tibet. This will take him seven years at least, possibly eight or nine, notwithstanding constant invocations. Seeing the Za corresponds in Christian experience with seeing God and becoming one with Him: "You are I and I am You."* During these years of seclusion his only communication with the outside world is through a small shutter in the wall of his room. His family may occupy a neighbouring room, but they may not disturb his meditation; more generally they live in a tent outside and go round with the Golokwa.

When he has seen the Za and at last leaves the cell, assured of the Za's support, the Agba is a person of great and peculiar power. If anyone strikes or otherwise insults him, he pulls down his long hair, shakes it three times, when fire comes out of it, and he calls on Za to punish the offender. Shortly afterwards the latter dies, or at least falls very sick. The Agba continues to live in the monastery. He dresses sometimes as an ordinary person and sometimes as a lama. In the bosom of his gown he carries a human skull-cup from which to drink. He carries also a trumpet and a purbu. The former is made from a human thigh-bone and should be covered with human skin, but sometimes yak- or sheep-skin is used. The purbu is a weapon like a dagger, its

* Union with God. There is an important difference in the two conceptions. Compare Jaeschke: "Saints continue their profound meditations for months and years, until the deity, finally overcome, stands before them visible and tangible, nay, until they have been personally united with and, as it were, incorporated into the invoked and subjected god." (*Dict.*, under "Lha-sgrub-pa," p. 121.) Also Sandberg: "By the tantrik system man gains by perseverance complete control over certain divine beings as well as demons, and uses them to accomplish his own will and fulfil his own wants. This power of coercion is drub-pa." (*Tibet*, p. 216.) Compare these with William James, who describes Christian saints as achieving a conviction, not merely intellectual, but as it were sensible, of the existence of an Ideal Power which they personify as God, as enjoying a sense of the friendly continuity of the Ideal Power with their own life, and a willing self-surrender to its control. (*Var. of Rel. Ex.*, p. 272, *et seq.*) In the one case the god is subjected to man, in the other man surrenders himself to God.

hilt consisting of a dorje surmounted by a demon's head, and its blade being three-edged. It hangs from the middle of the girdle and is used when invoking the Za against his enemies and to stab evil spirits. From the right side of his girdle hangs a human skin, which has been put through some softening process, and which he spreads on the floor before sitting down.

"Dsa-lung" means "artery-air" and denotes one who is able to make his body like air. No one who has not been a Yoga student can become a dsalungba, and most of the dsalungba are Nyimaba and Karjuba. Sitting in the "meditative attitude," the hermit concentrates all his thoughts on the non-existence of the body and practises self-levitation. At first he will not be able to rise in the air for more than half a foot but, with increased concentration, he can achieve ten feet. The period of meditation lasts for many years, the longer the better, and in due course miraculous powers are attained. The dsalungba is able to pass through a hole an inch in diameter; he can see what is happening on the other side of a wall or partition; he does not feel severe cold; and he can travel far and fast like the wind. When he dies he goes straight as an arrow to Dewajen. People say that a dsalungba can pass through a tiny aperture in the roof while still retaining the appearance of a full-grown man, and from the roof jump down on to a heap of barley without disturbing a single grain. But I have never met anyone who has actually seen this done. Once a man was pointed out to me as a dsalungba who had just taken a bath in a frozen river, and he came out with his body in a steam, apparently not feeling the cold.

And another time, when I was a small boy in Sikhim, I was witness in the Pedmayangtse lamasery of a strange incident which I have never been able to explain to my satisfaction. A lama came from the temple into the courtyard where we were standing and suddenly stamped his foot violently on the stone pavement. To the onlookers who enquired the reason for this action he explained that, when he came into the yard, he saw there a very bad spirit and so at once drove him out. His foot had left a print on the pavement like those of the five Panchen lamas shown at Drashilhunbo and it seemed to be about a quarter of an inch deep. This hermit lived not far from the Rumdig lamasery, two or three days distant from Pedmayangtse.

NOTE.—" Hermits who aspire to the sanctity of a Nal-jor (the Tibetan form of Yogi) go through three stages of meditation. The first is Da-wa, or Contemplation. The second is Gom-pa, or Complete Abstraction. The third and supreme position is that of Drub-pa, Consummation, and to reach this stage the devotee must acquire, and become a complete expert in, a certain physical process connected with the breath. This process is known as Arterial Absorption. It is part of Buddhist Tantrik science to believe and teach that the breath may be drawn in by numerous successive inspirations with as little expiration as possible, so as to be forced into the main arteries of the body. Practice, they allege, produces great expertness in holding in the breath and pumping it into the blood, when it causes a magical warmth and ecstatic giddiness in the head. Three conduits are supposed to proceed from the heart, and by this process the airy humour in the body known as RLUNG is said to be drawn from two of these—the RO-MA and the CHANG-MA—and forced into the centre one, WU-MA. It is when the *rlung* is in the *wuma* that a mystic heat is promoted throughout the whole frame, necessitating the gradual casting aside of every garment in the coldest weather. With this, meditation waxes hot likewise, and at length the intense mental concentration causes SEM—a vital elixir which nourishes the soul during its residence in the body—to pass also into the *wuma*, where it at once unites with the *rlung* present. That is the zenith of the process and at this stage the devotee is believed to be emancipated from the laws of gravity and to be able to expand and to contract his body to an indefinite extent, causing monstrous illusions to bystanders. The fit then subsides."—Sandberg, *Tibet and the Tibetans*, p. 281.

CHAPTER XIII

ON PILGRIMAGE WITH PEDMA RINCHEN—I.

By train to Budhgaya—The Temple and Bo Tree—Across Bhutan—The Migö—Milarasba's Temple—Lakes Yamdrog and Nam—Earnings on the Road—Lamas Barge and Mipam—We retrace our steps—Two Months with Headman Wednesday—Sand, Wind, and Poison Lakes—Bön Monasteries—The Ghosts' Rendezvous—Zhungru—First Sight of Holy Mountain.

THE lama and I went down the mountain by a small train to Siliguri, where we were to change for Budhgaya. It was evening, the station was lighted with great electric lights, and crowded with people, Europeans, Nepalese, Tibetans, Hindus, Mahomedans, and some Chinese, a very big place, so that Pedma Rinchen marvelled. I too wondered, although I had been accustomed to see electric lights at Darjeeling. Next morning we reached the Ganges, which was there two to three miles broad, and crossed by steam-launch, which was even more marvellous than the railway train. We were a party of seven Tibetans, men and women, and one Chinese, all making the pilgrimage to Budhgaya. On arriving at Budhgaya we were looked after by a Mahomedan, who was in charge of the temple, and who supplied us every morning with firewood and milk. Although the people were Hindus, their manner of living was like that of the Tibetans; they ate pea-tsamba, and sour milk, and huang-t'ang,* and burned cow-dung; but they called "Blighty"

* A Chinese word meaning "yellow sugar": Tib: buram, molasses.

after us,* because we were yellow, and wore Tibetan dress, and ate meat.

In the temple† is a big stone Buddha and outside are very many kinds of Buddhas, but all damaged, feet, hands, and noses broken. Those most damaged had been collected in a house by the Mahomedan caretaker, who had also repaired the others with plaster. There was a small lake with a wall round it, and between the wall and the lake many small cells, now empty. Buddha had lived there with his five hundred disciples, who bathed in the lake every morning. The lake is full of snakes and frogs, but it is said that the snakes do not harm anyone, as they have been blessed by Buddha's disciples and are very kindful. Between the lake and the temple is a tree under which Buddha spent six days.‡ There is also a big stone with two footprints of Buddha on it. Tibetan pilgrims bring pieces of cloth and saffron water and take impressions of the

* Strange to hear this word applied to Tibetan pilgrims! "Belati," I understand, is a corruption of the Hindustani word "wilayati," meaning "foreign"; and the substantive form "wilayat," corrupted into "belat," in Anglo-Indian slang, meant the country to which the British soldier went on leave. Tommies confused the adjective "belati" with the noun "belat," so England became "Blighty."

† The Temple. "The most holy of all sites, according to the lamas, in common with all Buddhists—like Mecca to the Mohamedans—is the Tree of Wisdom at Budhgaya in India, with its temple known to Tibetans as Gandhola, where Shakyamuni attained his Buddhahood, and which is believed to be the hub of the world." *Wadd.*, p. 306.

‡ "Bo Tree or Tree of Wisdom. This tree came to occupy much the same position among Buddhists as the Cross among Christians. Worship was actually paid to it, and an off-shoot is still growing on the spot where the Buddhist pilgrims found it, and where they believed the original tree had grown in the ancient temple at Bodh Gaya, near Rajgir, built about 500 A.D. by the celebrated Amara Sinha. A branch of it planted at Anuradhapura in Ceylon, in the middle of the third century B.C., is still growing there—the oldest historical tree in the world."—*R.D.*, p. 39. "The Mahavagga states that after attaining Buddhahood he sat cross-legged at the foot of the tree for seven days uninterruptedly, enjoying the bliss of emancipation, and while there thought out the chain of causation."—*Eliot*, I, 142.

footprints and pluck leaves from the tree. These they take home to Tibet and keep as charms. In the temple my lama lit several hundred butter lamps, and kotowed so many times and so hard that he got a big lump on his forehead. I also knelt with him and kotowed. No, I did not get a lump. After staying seven days we set out on our return journey; my lama was very happy and said: "If I die now, I am purified of all sins."

Arrived back at Darjeeling I did not go to the mission. The lama intended to visit holy mountains and monasteries and I wished to go with him, and he was glad of my company. He gave me a pair of good foreign boots and, after resting four days, we travelled by way of Pari to Badro in Bhutan, the residence of one of the two kings of Bhutan. The lama called on the king, who invited him to stay with him for one or two months, but we stayed only seven days. In a cave near Badro, called Dagtsang ("Tiger's Lair") or Badro-Dagtsang, the Mahaguru Pedma Sambhava lived for a time, and you can see the print of his back on the rock. This cave has a great name in Tibet.*

We then went on to Drongsa, in middle Bhutan, where lives the other king.† The lama called on him and was invited to stay for a few years. There

* Sherap adds that there is a similar cave at Kurje Bumtang, 15 miles east of Drongsa. In Bell's *Tibet* there is a photograph of the cave mentioned in the text.

† This was before the 1904 expedition to Tibet, after which the Penlop (Chief) of Drongsa became Maharaja of Bhutan. Previously there had been two kings, one spiritual, the Dharma Raja, who did not govern, and the other, also a priest, the Deb Raja, who in latter years himself ceased to govern. For at least 50 or 60 years the real power has lain with the Drongsa Penlop. Bhutan was not joined to the British Empire until 1910.—See *Bell*, p. 48.

According to Waddell, the capital of Bhutan and summer residence of the Grand Lama of Bhutan was Drashi-chöjong, which is about 15 miles east of Paro (Badro) as the crow flies.—*Wadd.*, p. 284.

are none of Geluba sect in Bhutan, mostly Nyimaba and some Karjuba*; and as Dsogchen Lamasery, where my lama, Pedma Rinchen, came from, is the centre of the Nyimaba and gives its name to the chief sub-sect, the king was very anxious to keep us.

But Pedma Rinchen did not like Bhutan, as the people are very wild. The men are fierce, and wear each three swords, which they are always ready to use; and the women are very lustful. Also the Bhutanese are very fond of giving people poison. The country is mountainous and the valleys are hot. The king offered to build a hermit's cell for the lama high up in the mountains, where it would be cool in summer, but the lama would not. We stayed with the king for two weeks, and he had a devil-dance in his courtyard, much the same as in Tibet, except that they did not know the dance and just made nonsense. The Bhutanese lamas are no good, they have all got Bhutan wives.

We left Bhutan by way of a high snow mountain, on the top of which is a cave called Sengedzong, or Monka Sengedzong, in which the Mahaguru lived for a time.† We spent the night in the cave. It was snowing heavily, very cold, and lonely. I could not sleep for the cold, and about midnight I heard the sound of someone moving in the dark. I called out "Lama! Lama!" but he whispered back, "Don't make noise: perhaps a robber." Leaving the cave next morning we saw the prints of very large bare feet in the snow, but there was no one about. After walking on for two or three hours we met many Bhutanese returning from Tibet and told

* Waddell states that only the Karju sect is represented in Bhutan, but Sherap maintains that this is quite incorrect.

† Sherap places this mountain to the east of Serkar Gutog.

them what had happened. They said at once, "It was a Migö," meaning "wild-man," I think a gorilla; there are many Migö in Bhutan.*

Two days after leaving the cave we entered Lhodrag, staying one night at the village of Kamding Lhakang, where you pay a bridge toll of half a tranka. Four days west is Serkar Gutog, where is a temple built by Milarasba, and in it is his wooden tsamba bowl, walking sticks, and the dress of Marba, his gegen; also the head-dress of Marba's wife. Both Marba and Milarasba were yogi.† The temple has nine storeys, and the top storey has a verandah, one foot wide, which pilgrims walk round in order to be purified of sin: very dangerful. I refused to go round. Lama said that if I fell down I should go straight to heaven, but if I did not go round I should still have sin. I said, "Never mind: if I fall down and die and become spirit, perhaps spirit go to hell: very dangerful, and twice have sorrow." So he went round alone.‡

* Mi—man; Gö—wild. Rockhill says that in Northern Tibet are heard many stories of hairy savages, with long, tangled locks falling around them like cloaks, naked, speechless beings, hardly human, who threw stones at travellers but who, having no arms, could do but little harm. He formed the conclusion that these were bears, which in that country are numerous and large. Their tracks, especially those of the hind paws, have some resemblance to those made by men with naked feet.—See *L. of L.*, pp. 116–7.

He also mentions (p. 150) the story of a Mongol who had seen what he called "wild men," who were covered with long hair, stood erect, and made tracks like men's, but he did not believe they could speak. He added that a Chinese who was with him when he saw them called out "Hsiung! Hsiung!" ("Bear! Bear!")

† Marba and his disciple Milarasba were founders of the Karju sect. Of Milarasba, the cotton-clad saint, poet, and miracle-worker, Eliot says that he "is perhaps the most picturesque figure in Lamaism, and in some ways reminds us of St. Francis of Assisi."—III, p. 399.

‡ This seems to be the edifice referred to as "Tse Gutog" by Major Bailey in the *Geographical Journal* of October, 1924. He says of it: "It is an act of great merit to walk round the narrow platform at the top of the tower, on which chains are tied for safety; but it required a better head for heights than we possessed."

Then we came after two days to a little temple from which you can see Lake Yamdrog. We did not go to the lake to visit Samding monastery, where Dorje Pamo lives, because we thought the boat too dangerous.* So on through nomad country full of wild horses to Lhoka valley, where St. Pedma Sambhava's Tibetan wife had a house, which is now in ruins. Passing over the Drag-la we reached Lhasa.

At Lhasa we stayed with a Dzongbön who was a friend of the lama, and after a few days set out again for Lake Nam. This is one of the lakes on which at daybreak you can see the Mahaguru's hand pressing down the devils that he had driven into the lake. Pedma Rinchen lay on the ground and looked along the white surface to see the dark impression of the hand and said that he thought he saw it ; but although I looked too at the same time, and very hard, I could not see anything. When the Saint came to Tibet he made four big lakes into which he drove the devils, and placed his hand on the water to keep them down. The names are Nam, Mapam, Yamdrog, and Chinghai.

From Namtso we went to Nagchuka and, as we intended crossing a very wild and uninhabited stretch of nomad country from there to Dsachuka, the lama purchased two horses, six yak, and a tent ; he also engaged a servant. Our object in visiting Dsachuka was to call on a very famous lama of the

* It would seem that Pedma Rinchen was under a misapprehension, as the monastery is not on an island. "Yamdok Lake is remarkable for its scorpionoid shape, the grotesque-shaped semi-island anchored to the main shore by two necks of land. Samding is itself placed on the main shore at the junction of the northern neck. Being built on a conical hill, it appears to be guarding the sacred island from intrusion."—*Wadd.*, p. 275. Perhaps the fact that Dorje Pamo is a tutelary of the Karju sect reconciled Pedma Rinchen to miss seeing Samding.

Nyima sect, called Barge lama. It took us two months to get to Dsachuka. The road was sometimes full of nomads, at other times we might see no one for ten days. There were a good many robbers, but they did not molest us, partly out of respect for the lama, partly because they did not consider us worth robbing. As a matter of fact we made a good deal of money on that road. Lamas were scarce, and we were constantly being begged by nomads to stop and read prayers to them and to baptise children, "give them power," as it is called. I acted as the lama's assistant, and when the nomads gave him ten rupees they would give me five. Travelling thus, I learned from the lama a great deal about the beliefs of the Nyimaba.

Arrived at Dsachuka we found that Barge lama had died, and that his place had been taken by another lama called Mipam. Mipam was like Barge lama in every respect. They were the most learned lamas in Tibet. Living as hermits in caves they dressed like beggars and, while they made many books, they all the time preached to the people just like foreign missionaries. Both of them came from Dsogchen. The lama stayed with Mipam for one month, discussing religion and exchanging experiences. Mipam told Pedma Rinchen that he should visit K'unlun.* Being now so near home the lama was not anxious to go back and make such a long journey north, but Mipam said that he must go, as it was the holiest mountain in Tibet, so eventually he agreed.

At Mipam's request the nomads supplied us with plenty of butter, cheese, tea, dried meat,

* Sherap means Mount Kailas: see note on p. 166.

and a little tsamba for the road, also one or two yak. We turned back to go through Nagchuka; but, as the nomads on that road now knew the lama, so many asked him to stop and read books and give power that it took us three months to reach Nagchuka. From there we went west to Dalung lamasery, about six days' journey; and there we stayed in the hope that traders expected from Lhasa would arrive with tsamba, since Dalung had no good food itself, and was the last place at which we had a chance of getting tsamba for a long time. Luckily we had not to wait more than a few days before the traders arrived, and we purchased half a load. We then travelled north-west round Nyen Chen Tang La and back a little south to Yangbachen; then on to the north side of Bangba Bayang.

Here at the request of a rich young nomad chief called Lhagba, the lama stopped for one month. Lhagba, which means Wednesday, was the name given to the chief when a baby, because he was born on a Wednesday, and there was no lama near to give him power; and although he had afterwards been baptised Drashi Dserin, still everyone continued to call him Genbo Lhagba, that is Headman Wednesday. After we had been with him for one month, our host and all the young people had to take the yak to the grasslands, and it was decided that the lama should go with them while I should stay behind in the big tent with the aged uncle and one servant. They were away for one month, by which time they had exhausted the pasturage in that place and came back to set out for a fresh one. While they were away there was nothing for me to do, yet I never tired of watching the wild life in the neighbourhood of the camp, wild horses, wild yak, wild sheep, wild goats, and duck in great number. On one small lake, and there were very many, there might be a thousand duck ; and I could not sleep at night for the noise of the ducks and trung-trung (cranes). Also, although the grass on the plain was not very good, it was studded with many tiny flowers. After the young people had come back, we prepared to continue our journey. We left our yaks and our tent and other things with our host, to keep for our return, and also dismissed our servant. We kept only two sheep, large animals, to carry our food and clothes.

From Bangba Bayang we went to Bangba Chugdso, which also is full of wild animal life ; but the country is very poor. Of course there are no roads. We took the direction roughly by the sun, and enquired the way of such people as we met. The going is very difficult on account of the sand, especially in the afternoon when strong winds get up. So our travelling was done mainly in the morning, when there was usually a blue sky. We averaged about thirty or forty *li* a day, never doing more than fifty.* Water was another difficulty, as we found that the lakes were all salt. Tibetans call them Poison Lakes, and say that if you drink of them you die, or at least become very sick. We had to buy a sheep's stomach in which to carry water. One very large lake is called Dangra Yutso, on the north side of a snow mountain called Dargo, and we struck it on the eastern shore. The religion of the Chugdso people is Bön. Their staple food is wild horse and goat. We lived in tents when we could get them,

* The Chinese *li* is about one-third of an English mile.

although they are very small, and five or six people crowd them. Yak-dung makes excellent fuel, giving out great heat, but in a tent it is hard on the eyes. Mount Dargo is regarded by the Bön as a very holy mountain. It has one or two small lamaseries at its foot, and the lama called there; but as all the talk was of Bön, in which he had no great interest, he did not like it very much. We then went to the south side of the mountain where is a rather larger Bön lamasery, with fifty or sixty monks. The monastery is well built, and its houses are prettily painted inside, and here we found plenty of tsamba and everything to buy. About five miles farther on is a little village, Yönchödengga, where many people from Tsang, Sachya, and Lhadse, beyond Sachya, come to trade, selling grain for salt, sheep, and yak. We were now a month's journey from Dalung, and we stayed here for several days, bathing in the hot sulphur springs, and buying good mutton and beef.

We then went round to the north-west side of Dargo to Bangba Gedse, where is a big salt lake called Drabye, which produces salt for all Tibet. Then to Darjeling monastery, which houses a few hundred lamas of the yellow sect, where we stayed for two days. Having obtained a further supply of butter, cheese, and dried meat, we went to Lower Droshü, then across the river to a place in Nepal called Chumijadsa, where is a small lamasery. Round the lamasery temple are 128 small springs, not hot, and inside it a large spring burning all the time with blue fire; the ground round the spring is also alight. It is said that this is the meeting-place of all the Dre. Lamas who live here for nine years, nine months, and nine days, get on friendly terms with the Dre, and are, therefore, regarded as powerful intermediaries. But living is difficult on account of the scarcity of food. Pedma Rinchen stayed six weeks ; and every night, since the Dre come at night, he took his big drum, his bell, and thigh-bone trumpet and did chöba work, calling the Dre and talking with them. I was afraid to go there by night. The men and women of this place look like an aboriginal tribe, and indeed "Lo," in which Chumijadsa is situated, means "aborigines." They are poorly dressed and generally go barefoot. They wear the hair long, coiled round the top of the head, and they stick it full of sewing needles in order, it is said, to frustrate enemies who try to catch them by the hair. The country is under the Nepal Government.

We then came back across the river to Zhungru, a small community between Upper and Lower Droshü. The official is a nomad, appointed by the Dalai Lama, and called Shebön. He became very fond of the lama. Being sick he had wanted a lama to read to him and give him power, so he was very glad when Pedma Rinchen appeared. The Shebön so much praised the lama to others that two or three hundred people came for favours, and for two days we were very busy. They gave us sheep, dried meat, butter, and money ; and the women gave their ear-rings. In fact we got far more food than we could possibly carry, so that the lama offered it to the official ; but the latter would not accept without paying for it, and gave him some fifty or sixty trankas.

We then went on to the Namjel Lhadse (Sachya) monastery in Upper Droshü, a small place where we stayed in order to see the Soda (Püto) Lake and the Tsala mine. Soda is all round the side of the lake like flowers, and lies on the water like ice. It is very troublesome when the wind blows. Nomads take it away in yak-skins for sale to Tibetans, who use it in washing clothes and also in making tea in order to bring the colour out.

Next morning we set out again, and after a few days we reached the grassy plateau of Mayum-la, down which flows the Horse River (Tsangbo), and from the middle of which we could see the snowy top of Mount K'unlun,* "the navel of Tibet." On sighting the sacred mountain Pedma Rinchen knelt in prayer and was very happy. We went downhill to another turquoise lake (yutso) called Mapam.† It is one of those on which you are supposed to see the Guru's hand, but neither I nor Pedma Rinchen could make it out. Near it is a small Sachya monastery, in which we stayed.

I should mention that although the Horse River is said to have its source in the Mayum-la, we did not see its springs.

* Sherap had all along referred to this mountain as K'unlun; and it was only when tracing the pilgrimage on a map and coming to a halt at Mayum-la, some three degrees of latitude south of K'unlun, that I realised that he must be talking of another mountain, which was identified when he said that the Indians called it "Klass" (Kailas) and Pedma Rinchen called it Gangar Dise or Gang Rinboche. Edkins says: "Some (Chinese geomancers) adopt the Hindu nomenclature, and make the Sumeru Mountain the centre of the mountain and river system of the world. Others, who object to offer so great a concession to the foreign doctrine of Buddhist books, prefer to assign this honour to Kwun-lun, the old Chinese name of the mountains dividing Tibet from Tartary. On the north side of these mountains the Chinese probably resided for a time before proceeding to take possession of their present home."—*Chinese Buddhism*, p. 336. "Kailas, styled Gang Tise by Tibetans, has a central summit measured trigonometrically at 21,830 feet."—*Sandberg*, p. 270.

† Lake Mapam is the holy lake Manasarovara.—*Jaeschke*, p. 265.

CHAPTER XIV

ON PILGRIMAGE WITH PEDMA RINCHEN—II.

Different Cures for Knee Trouble—Indian Pilgrims—Koko Nor Legend—Drölma-la—The Young Woman in the Red Gown—Legends of Milarasba—A Hermit's Tsamba-bowl—Gedmo Dagjel—Fairs—The Burong Buddha—Through Kurnu to Ladak—The Floating Island at Lahore—To Nepal—The Jirong Jowo—Chöden of Yombu—Impudent Monkeys—Jadsima's Petticoat—Gyangtse.

THREE days after our arrival in the Sachya monastery something went wrong with my knees, so that I could hardly walk. Pedma Rinchen attributed my sickness to a devil, and read books to me, and gave me fruit and tsamba which he had blessed, but all was no good ; I got worse and could not stand. As the holy mountain was only five days distant, the lama left me in charge of the priest and started off for it. The priest was a Ladak man, a skilful doctor. He brought me some medicine which looked like mud, rubbed it on my knees, and bandaged them with yak-hair. He then tied a rope horizontally across the room, and told me to hold on to it and practice walking. The result was that seven days after my lama had left I was well again.

After being away fourteen days Pedma Rinchen returned, having circumambulated the mountain, and next morning we started off together, arriving after five days at the village of Darchen at the foot of the mountain, having passed through Barka Dazam and waded a small river. Next morning, however, my knees were bad again and I did not get well for fifteen days. During this time the lama circumambulated the mountain three times: it takes four or five days to go round. Fortunately some Indians were in the village who, when they learned that I spoke Hindustani, were very kind to me. I had my meals with them. After each meal they always were careful to wash their brass bowls and scour them with mud. They insisted on doing the same with my wooden tsamba bowl, from which, as we had three meals a day, the pretty varnish was soon worn off and the bowl spoiled in appearance. The Indians addressed the holy mountain "Klass! Klass!" raising their hands to it. The Tibetan name is Gang Rinboche, the Precious Mountain, or, Gang Gar Dise, White Mount Dise.

Near the top of the mountain on the Darchen side, Pedma Rinchen pointed out to me a small black patch among the snow where the Guru Pedma Sambhava had picked up earth with which to stop the overflow of the spring at Koko Nor. When the Guru lived on Dise, Koko Nor did not exist; there was only a spring, from which nomads in the vicinity drew water. After water was drawn, they were always careful to put a cover over the spring's mouth, either to keep out impurities or to prevent it from overflowing. One evening, however, a woman who had gone for water forgot to replace the cover, with the result that the spring overflowed and formed a vast lake, in which 10,000 families were drowned. Learning of the disaster the Guru picked up a handful of earth from the mountain and, hurling it at Koko Nor, stopped up the spring and formed a small hill in the middle of the lake. The name of the hill and of the lamasery afterwards built on it is Tsonying Mahadewya, that is, the great god in the middle of the lake, and the lake itself is called Yutso Trishog Jelmo, Lake of Ten Thousand Families, Queen of Lakes. Then the Guru put his hand on the lake to repress the evil spirit that had caused the overflow. As there are no boats on the lake, the lamasery is in touch with the mainland only in winter when the lake is frozen over ; and then the lamas have to lay in a stock of wood and food to carry them over next summer. Koko Nor in Chinese is Ching Hai.*

The lama took me round the mountain. Two days west from Darchen is Drölma-la, the Goddess of Mercy Mountain. Near the road is a big, flat rock, very oily in appearance, with human hair and bones scattered over it. It is the rock on which pilgrims that die on the road are exposed to the vultures ; and, not pilgrims only ; corpses are brought here from Barka and Darchen ; so there are always plenty of them, and some are eaten and some not. The spirits of pilgrims who die on pilgrimage go straight to Dewajen.

On the top of this peak is a big, square rock, crowned with prayer flags, and called the House of the Twenty-one Drölmas. On it are many wolves' footprints ; and it is said that the twenty-one Drölmas appeared there in wolves' bodies. Underneath the rock is a small cave in which was sleeping a young woman in a red gown. Beside her was an

* Rockhill gives another version of the legend. "This rocky island, it is said, fills the orifice through which the waters of the lake rushed out when they came by a subterranean passage from Lhasa to the Kokonor country. It was brought there by a god who had taken the shape of a great bird, and by this timely expedient had saved the country from being entirely submerged."—*L. of L.*, p. 123.

Huc gives an account of the origin of the lake substantially the same as the above.—II, p. 176, *et seq.*

earthenware pot with some frozen water in it, and near by were many human bones. She also had many foreign needles, and she asked us for needles. Pedma Rinchen offered her half a tranka and some tsamba and some dried turnip, which is a good thing to eat when crossing high passes,* but she refused them and still demanded needles. It was common talk that she ate human flesh and gnawed human bones; and some said that she was a devil, and some that she was a goddess; but for me I do not know. I enquired of her whence she came and she replied "Chamdo," in Kam; and I would have enquired further what she did there in the cave, but my mind was full of the stories and, seeing the human bones, my stomach was turned, and I felt too sick to ask questions. Yet, she was comely in appearance, and her face plump and of good colour.

Half a day from there we saw another rock with human footprints on it. Here, it is said, Milarasba met a Bön pilgrim going the opposite way. Each tried to drag the other in what he considered the proper direction; hence the numerous footprints.† Another half day farther on is a cave with a slab of rock for roof. On the roof are footprints, and underneath, on the ceiling as it were, are the marks of a man's head and his two hands. Milarasba went to live in this cave, and as it was too low, he pushed it up with his head and two hands; he pushed

* Dried Turnip. Rockhill says that garlic is held to be an antidote for the pestilential vapours that are supposed to come out of the soil in high altitudes, and that cause giddiness, nausea, and other indications of rarefied air.—*L. of L.*, p. 149.

† Mount Dise used to be in the possession of the Bönbo. When Milarasba went there, he claimed it as the inheritance of the Buddhists. The Bön priest to whom he made the claim proposed that they compete for it by feats of jugglery. They did so, and Milarasba won.—See *Sandberg*, p. 270.

too high, so walked on the roof to press it down again.

A day farther on we saw, high up on the mountain, a hermit's retreat. We had heard that a very holy lama of the Dsogchen sect, a native of Amdo, lived there. Climbing up, we found the entrance of the cave curtained round by a wall which had in it a very small aperture blocked by a stone. At our knock the hermit came out. He had long hair in which were many rosaries, was clad in a green gown, not of lama cut, and carried a thigh-bone trumpet; in his right hand was an axe, which he afterwards hung at his girdle. He enquired where we came from and what we wanted, and learning that the lama was from Derge Dsogchen, invited us in and prepared tea for us. He also made tsamba, but it was mixed with juniper leaves and so nasty that Pedma Rinchen and I made ours up into a ball and threw it away when we got outside. For about two hours the hermit and the lama talked on religion and of the Dsogchen lamas they had known, and while they talked I went out into the little yard at the entrance of the cave. It was hung with human hair, human skins, skulls, and the bones of hands; also many women's breasts hung on a rope, like a clothes-line, having become quite hard; the hermit had obtained them from the rock at Drölma-la. The tsamba bowl that he used was the skin of a woman's breast, kept soft by some process, and in it he mixed tsamba, tea, and dry cheese. The bowls he gave us were of wood.

On our return to Darchen we received a visit from the famous robber chief Dagjel, whom I have already mentioned in connection with the nomads of Adra Dsamar. He had a following of fifteen tents, and came to invite the lama to visit him in his camp at Barka Dazam, to read books and tell his fortune. The lama and I circumambulated the mountain once again. This made the lama's sixth trip. After his first tour he had intended to make twelve altogether, but he was now tired; also we could not get firewood or yak-dung on the road and could not make tea; so he thought that six times was enough, and we went down to Darchen and on to Barka Dazam. This is a village of some ten or a dozen houses where Tibetan tea-traders do business. We were the robber chief's guests for three days, reading books, giving power, calculating his fortune, and praying to the good spirit of Dise and to the bad spirit of a neighbouring peak. The traders in the village invited us to spend three or four days with them and Pedma Rinchen did not call on the Dzongbön because he was afraid that he would be delayed still longer. We were loaded with the usual presents of food.

The next stage was to Janyima, four days. On the third day we saw the source of the Peacock River. At Janyima an annual fair is held in summer time which nomads, Indians, and Lhasa people attend. The Indians bring "dickjes," huang-tang, sewing machines, etc., and trade them for the usual Tibet and China goods. Here we saw five or six Europeans, who were in the neighbourhood duck shooting.* After spending a week at Janyima we went on three days to Burong. Here is the Shenbeling, with a few hundred lamas of the Geluba. The

* A few years later, by the Trade Regulations of 1908 (Art. 9), British subjects were definitely barred from travelling in Tibet beyond the trade marts of Gyangtse, Yatung, and Gartok.

monastery is built on a mountain, the sides of which are perforated with many caves, having little shacks at the entrance ; these are inhabited. In the Shen-beling is one of the three brother Buddhas, the two others being in the Jokang at Lhasa, and at Jirong, in Nepal. The Jokang Buddha fell down from heaven, while the two others were turned up out of the earth during ploughing, and have a mark on the forehead where the plough struck. The Burong Buddha is quite small, perhaps only three feet. Pedma Rinchen lighted butter lamps and prayed. In front of the monastery is a big plain on which is held an annual fair like that at Janyima. Burong is a poor country, no trees, wretched grass, yellow mountains.

Pedma Rinchen was anxious to go to Lahore, in the Punjab, to see the place where the rival suitors bound the Guru Pedma Sambhava on the pyre, when the Guru was seen seated on a lotus flower in the midst of the flames. On enquiry we learned that we had to go back to Janyima and then on through Jakargo and Dretaburi. This we did, and found it to be wild country with no houses and few nomads. From Dretaburi we went north-west to Arijong, near the Ladak border, and thence south to Kurnu. Kurnu is a warm and fertile country where you can procure anything you want. The people are half-caste, a mixture of Tibetans and Indians, and their speech also is a mixture. They spend much money on good works, pilgrimages, etc. From Kurnu we went north-west into Ladak, in the state of Kashmir, a yellow country, very poor There we stayed for about a week at a Sachya monastery called Lhundrub Gomba, whose kanbo had travelled a good deal, having visited Derge, Kam, and India. Dried peaches were plentiful, but not much else in the way of food; we had peach porridge every day. We then went on to the capital Leh, a poor place, and the people stupid. They wear long, white, woollen gowns down to the ankle. I was told that there was a German mission there, but Pedma Rinchen would not let me call, as he said that by doing so I should lose all the merit that I had acquired by my pilgrimage.

North-west of Leh is the country of Urgyan,* where the blind king reigned who first saw the Guru on the lotus.† But it would have taken almost a month to get there, so we went through the Bati country (where the people talk a language I did not know and go almost naked) to Zahor or Lahore, which is twenty days from Leh. In Lahore is a small lake, perhaps 200 feet wide, with a tiny island in it on which are three trees, one fairly large, with a smaller one on either side. The large one is Mahaguru and the smaller ones his two wives. It was said that before sunrise the island moves round the lake; people go there and light butter lamps and pray to the three trees. I did not see the island go round, but it did seem to me to move a little during a high wind. I thought that perhaps there might be a wooden platform underneath it.‡

We came back through Kurnu, Burong, and Droshü to Namjel Lhadse. Arrived there, the lama proposed to visit the three big pagodas of Nepal,

* Urgyan, i.e. Udyana.—*Wadd.*

† See below, p. 183.

‡ Huc describes "floating islands" on the P'ing Hu, in Hupei, China: these were rafts of bamboo carrying fields and houses, with sails set on the houses and at each corner of the "island."—*Chinese Empire*, II, ch. 3.

so we went south-east to Dsong Gar village, near the Nepal border, where are some big lamaseries and many lamas of the Geluba, not farms or trees but much trade. Between Dsong Gar and Nepal is the country where Milarasba was born, and it is full of holy places with which he was connected. Then to Jirong, a small town in Nepal. In Jirong Valley, about a mile north-west of the town of Jirong, is a big temple with a very large Jamba or Maitreya, made of mud and standing fifty or sixty feet high. It sits, foreign fashion, with hands on knees, and you have to climb up stairs to see the face.

Jirong town has a mixed population of something over one hundred families—Tibetans, Nepalese, and half-castes—and a temple with a famous statue of Buddha, known as the Jirong Jowo, that is, the Lord of Jirong. This Buddha, and those at Burong and in the Jokang, are the most renowned in Tibet. I do not know what the Jokang Buddha is made of, but it is covered with gold wash. The two at Jirong and Burong are made of metal, only the face being gold washed; and they are small, about three feet high. They were none of them made by human hands; the Jokang Buddha fell from heaven,* while those at Burong and Jirong were dug up alive while ploughing, the plough making a wound on the forehead.

After a stay of two or three days in Jirong we went to Yombu, one of the two capitals of Nepal,† separated only by a mile from the other, Yirong. A little to the north-west of Yombu is a small artificial

* Another legend tells that it was brought to Tibet by Princess Wên Ch'êng when she married King Songdsengombo.—*Wadd.*, p. 303.

† Yombu, i.e. Khatmandu.

hill covered with trees, in which live many monkeys. On the top of the hill is a very large chöden, the lower half of which is underground. Entering by a small door you first descend to the place where the body of Nagarjuna (Ti-ludu) is supposed to be kept, but we could not see it anywhere. In this large and damp-smelling vault little white pills are sold, which are alleged to be made from Nagarjuna's bones, and eating which you may be saved from hell; but they are rather expensive, a tranka each. The chöden is called Pagba Shing-gun* and, including the hill in which it is partly buried, is perhaps 200 feet high. Round it are the houses of the lamas; and everything has to be kept under cover on account of the monkeys, which are very audacious. They steal fruit from the open baskets of passers-by, and go into the temple and lamas' houses, blow out the lamps and lick up the butter. West of this chöden is a high, well-wooded mountain, a little like an elephant in shape, and therefore called the Langri Lungden. Buddha frequently went there, and a stone seat which he used remains to this day.

Two or three miles north of Yombu is another very big chöden built of stone and mud a long time ago by an old woman known as Jadsima. The chöden's name is Jarong Kasho.† It is not quite so big as the Pagba Shing-gun and has no entrance. Its cone is gold-washed. A Chinese lama is in charge, and round the chöden are plenty of houses for the use of pilgrims. Many Tibetan pilgrims go

* Svayambhunath Stupa.—*Wadd.*, p. 315.

† Maguta Stupa. It attracts far more votaries than the Pagba Shing-gun, and is the chief place of Lamaist pilgrimage in Nepal. The story of Jadsima, printed in booklet form, is sold at the stupa.—*Wadd.*, *ibid.*

there in winter. They make rice-beer, for the country is warm and people thirsty, and give it away to the Nepalese as a "good work." Nepalese women wear the skirt, which is "gathered," long in front and tucked up behind. This is because the old woman, the fowl-keeper, who built the chöden with her own hands, had no basket, and carried the stones and mud for building in the skirt of her dress, tucking it up behind to enable her to use the lap for this purpose.

We stayed at Jarong Kasho for two weeks. Two days east of Yombu* is another chöden, quite small. The Buddha, who has lived five hundred times, was in one reincarnation born son of the king of Nepal. As a good work he gave his body to a hungry tiger, his bones afterwards being collected and deposited in this chöden, the name of which is Dagmo Lüjin, that is, "gift of body to tigress." We spent two days there before returning to Jarong Kasho, and visited many other holy places, including Yirong, where is a small temple with a Drölma (Tara) of silver, about life-size. The people worship the Drölma by killing goats, chickens, and doves, and pouring the blood at her feet. In Yirong they make many "dickjes" and cymbals for sale in Tibet. We stayed just an hour or two.

Without delaying at Jirong we went straight back to Bangba Bayang and collected the various things that we had left in the custody of Headman Wednesday; one of our yaks had died. From Bangba Bayang we visited Drashilhunbo, the capital of Tsang, with its five temples and five chöden, and spent one or two days there before going on to

* Waddell says, about 12 miles from Khatmandu.—*Ibid.*

Gyangtse, but we lodged in Shigatse, as lamas who are not of the established church are not allowed to stay in Drashillunbo overnight. By this time Pedma Rinchen was becoming tired of travelling. At Gyangtse a friend named Serchog, who was a Tibetan official, begged him to stay with him as a hermit for a few years and read sacred books to him, to which the lama agreed. I also stayed with Serchog for one year. He was extremely kind to me, but I was anxious to go back to Sikhim, and as he did not wish me to go there, I was obliged to lie to him and said that I must go to Budhgaya and other holy places in India. He presented me with money, about sixty taels*; and let me go. So I returned to Gangtog.

* About £9.

CHAPTER XV

THE DEVIL DANCE AT TACHIENLU (DARTSENDO).

(An Address delivered to the Border Research Society, Chêngtu, 1st December, 1924.)

WHEN at Tachienlu this summer I had the good fortune to fall in with a Tibetan who had travelled much, and who, having sharp eyes, a keen interest in everything he saw about him, a retentive memory, and a knowledge of English, was able to give me, during the three months I spent there, some very interesting information regarding the manners and customs of the people. For an hour or two every evening Mr. Sherap discoursed on this subject, and when, towards the end of my stay, he had exhausted his store of observations and reminiscences, I was more or less prepared to appreciate the part played in Tibetan life by such religious ceremonials as the so-called "Devil-Dance." Handicapped by ignorance of the language, I am indebted to the Rev. R. Cunningham, of the China Inland Mission at Tachienlu, for revising my romanisation of Tibetan words and transcribing them phonetically according to the Lhasa dialect.

* * * * * *

The plot and motive of "The Mystery Play of Tibet" seem never to have been definitely ascertained, owing doubtless to the cumbrous details which so thickly overlay it and the difficulty of finding competent interpreters of the plot, as well as the conflicting accounts current amongst the lamas themselves in regard to its origin and meaning.

Thus Waddell, the authority on "Lamaism," and in spite of his efforts and those of previous writers to disentangle meaning and personality among the apparently incoherent mob of masked figures, the mystification still exists to fascinate every traveller to Tibet. So when I learned that the Dorje Drag lamasery, a Nyima foundation situated about one mile outside the town, proposed to hold a devil-dance, I instructed Sherap to get into touch with the lamas, and from the actors themselves discover its meaning. He endeavoured to do so, but brought back the disappointing report that the dances were performed in accordance with traditional custom and were in honour of Saint Pedma Sambhava; there was no "book of words"; and while the designation of the dancers was known, and what they were expected to do, the reference behind the impersonation was seldom realised, the special as distinct from the general significance of the performances having been forgotten. The particular lama who, being a tall fellow, was to take the leading rôle, that of Purba, admitted that he did not know what much of it was about. "For example," he enquired pertinently, "why introduce a cowherd and his wife?"

The Badsi are certainly somewhat ridiculous creatures and seem very much out of place, although they supply a comic element in what would otherwise be an entirely gruesome business. Both are fresh from the country, what I believe the Americans would call "Rubes," with straw in their hair, so to speak; and they wander about the courtyard, trying every now and then to milk their cow, and offering a spoonful to Pedma Sambhava in his several forms.

As a matter of fact, the Saint has got a long memory and exacts homage from those who were enemies in his earthly life. He does not forget that, when he was at Lahore, he won the affections of a beautiful princess who, deeming none of her suitors worthy of her hand, had retired to a nunnery; and that their amours were spied upon by a cowherd and his wife, who carried the tale to the king; whence much trouble.*

Nor does he forget Hashang, the fat man, who is known to every foreigner in China as "The Laughing Buddha," whose brass or porcelain figure is bought in the foreign market as a mascot, and who represents Maitreya. But historically Hashang is identified with the Chinese priest, ho-shang, who tooth and nail contested Pedma Sambhava's teaching, who denied that the wizardry of Kashmir had anything in common with Gautama's message, and who, as one of the Saint's most bitter enemies, was eventually expelled from Tibet.† He, too, figures in the dance as paying homage to the Maha Guru; it is he, in fact, whose proper part it is to present to his former enemy, now recognised as "The Second Buddha," the "Eight Glorious Offerings."‡

* Sherap is my authority for the cowherd story. For the nature of the "trouble," see p. 173.

† For the identification of Hashang with Maitreya's last incarnation, see *Wadd.*, p. 378, and with the Chinese priest (ho-shang) who was expelled by St. Pedma, *ib.*, pp. 31 and 534.

‡ The Eight Glorious Offerings were originally presented to Buddha by Brahma, Indra, and others, and blessed by him.—See *Wadd.*, p. 393.

These stories may be forgotten by illiterate lamas, but the dance continues to follow the tradition of centuries. Perhaps the head lama in the monastery knew the exact significance of each of the cast, for he was old and reputedly erudite; perhaps, as Sherap suggested, he feigned ignorance lest, if he imparted to foreigners the secrets of his religion, he should incur the wrath of Purba. However that may be, and I incline personally to the illiteracy theory, after a long and patient inquisition among lamas and laymen of all sorts, not unaccompanied by *douceurs* and "refreshers," although still many of the masks remain mere names, their special significance undetermined, yet on the whole a fairly comprehensive and coherent account of this particular play was obtained.

Of course much of the fearsome quality that attaches to the devil-dance is due to the mystification of the onlooker. *Omne ignotum pro magnifico* observed Tacitus, in explanation of the panic of the troops the night before they went "over the top" into Caledonia; and the epigram is particularly apposite to phenomena like the devil-dance. For after following the rehearsals of the performance and being coached in what to expect when at last the play is staged, instead of having the mind purged by terror and pity, as Aristotle would have it, one is inclined to be increasingly critical of both the dance and the dancers, and finally to charge the demons with downright amateurishness, for which after all many of the poor devils are not to be blamed, considering the shortness of the call to play that rôle.

The festival begins on the 10th day of the 7th

moon, which fell this year on 10th August, the anniversary of the day on which, Waddell informs us, the blind king of Udyana found on the pure bosom of the sacred Lake of Kusha a lotus flower of matchless beauty, on whose petals sat a lovely boy of eight years old, sceptred and shining like a god, who was come in accordance with the prophecy of Shakyamuni to deliver all beings from misery, and whose name was Pedma Sambhava, the lotus-born.

The morning of the 10th broke fine; and about 9 o'clock we joined the happy throng that wandered leisurely out of town and up alongside the mountain torrent to Dorje Drag. The level sward in front of the lamasery was already covered with tents, the Tibetans being quite unable to resist the idea of a picnic; and the brightly-striped canvas and gaily-coloured clothes of men and women made a pretty picture against the rows of sombre poplars in the background. As we wended our way through the crowd, now and then one more polite than his neighbours would stand aside, bow with outstretched hands, and protrude a tongue of monstrous size and usually healthy colour, the polite form of salutation in Tibet. At a stall near the lamasery gateway we found a friend of ours, a modern George Borrow, busily handing out Christian tracts to the curious. When I mention that this picturesque figure was clad in a blue Chinese gown, wore straw sandals and no hat, you will have no difficulty in recognising a F.R.G.S. who is an esteemed member of this Society.

Passing through the vestibule with its great Mani drums, revolved by devotees as they go by, and entering the courtyard, we saw stretched opposite to us, concealing the entrance to the main temple, an enormous painting on cloth of Pedma Sambhava. On all four sides of the yard the verandahs and galleries of the lamás' dormitories up to the third storey were a blaze of colour, Chinese and Tibetan ladies vying with each other in the display of fine clothes and glittering jewellery. With their usual courtesy the Chinese officials had placed at my disposal a room alongside theirs in one of the upper storeys, but on Sherap's advice I had taken care to book one on the ground floor. It was as well that I had done so, for during the first day of the dance the whole courtyard was protected from the sun by a thick awning, and persons who at first were disposed to congratulate themselves upon being elevated above the *profanum vulgus*, were obliged to descend the stairs in order to see what was happening under the awning. The room we used as a "box" (for a fee of $10) was on the same side of the courtyard as the entrance, and it faced the Saint's picture from the temple, behind which the dancers emerged.

Unfortunately for the lamasery, the date of the ceremony coincided this year with political trouble, the Border Commissioner taking advantage of a temporary truce with his enemies of Szechuan to proceed to Peking in order to lay his case before the President of the Republic. Unable to use the Szechuan route, he had tried to go south through Yunnan, but the Governor there proved unexpectedly hostile and he was obliged to come back to Tachienlu and try the north road through the country of the wild Golok. As he was looked for at any moment, all the officials, with perhaps the single exception of the Magistrate, had left town on horseback to meet him on the other side of the Jedo. Consequently the scene in the lamasery was deprived of much of its accustomed pomp and splendour, and the lamas of not a little profit also, for each official who honours the occasion with his presence is expected to contribute liberally, not only for the "boxes" provided them, but also by way of presents of brick-tea for the use of the lamasery. This particular performance suffered further from the fact that many of the lamas were absent on pilgrimage to Lhasa and on business in the Mi-nyag country, so that the cast was considerably depleted, the participants numbering only ninety-four, inclusive of the band, instead of considerably over one hundred. To my personal regret Hashang, whom I had particularly looked forward to seeing, was one of those cut out of the programme; but I might have been disappointed in him, as I understand that he does not always appear in his fat form. Sherap, in fact, tells me that he has never heard of his supposed connection with Maitreya, the authority for which is Waddell.

The number of dances or acts is eleven, six on the first and five on the second day. The first four are not devil-dances in the strict sense of the word: the participants are celestial beings come to pay homage to the Saint. The fifth act is merely an introduction to the sixth, wherein the terrible Gönbo Ma-Ning arrives and, with fourteen attendant demons, dances in honour of the Guru. Similarly the seventh and eighth are occupied with the advent of the still more redoubtable Purba, with his bird-faced janitors and other strange-looking demons;

but while these two dances are going on, the chief wizard is occupied in compelling into the Ling-ga the devils that during the past year have broken their promise to the Saint and done their best to destroy his religion. In the Ninth and Tenth "The Stag" cuts up and eats the Ling-ga, distributing portions of it also to Purba and his followers; I was unable to learn why this duty was allotted to a stag. In the final act the sacrificial dorma and the dorma invested with evil spirits are carried down to the river-edge and burned with much "beating of the drum."

DRAMATIS PERSONÆ.

(Arranged in Alphabetical Order.)

ADSARA, 2, demonic attendants on the Gönbo Ma-Ning. They wear a wooden helmet with flags on it, and a short gown.

AGBA, the chief wizard: black hat surmounted by peacock feather fan; richly embroidered robes; carries purbu in right and skull-cup in left hand; is provided with special tent in courtyard, to which he retires periodically to rest from his spirit-calling activities. Two other Agba accompany the Gönbo. The Zhanag (*q.v.*) are also Agba. All agba carry purbu and skull-cup.

BADSI, 2, cowherd and his wife, with their cow: the man carries a sling, the woman a milk-pail.

BAMO, 5, also called GADROMA, goddesses from Lha, consorts of the Bawo, highest conception of female beauty: wear the Jelwa Rignga (p. 189) and carry drums; part is taken by small boys.

BAWO, 5, in Chinese "chün-tzu," spirits of heroes from Lha.

DRAJE, 10, demonic attendants of Purba, in bird- and other animal-masks: carry axe and sword.

DRASHIDSEJE, 8 masks representing the Eight Glorious Offerings, namely, the Mirror, Calculus, Milk Curds, Darba Grass, Cocoa-nut, Conch Shell, Minium and Sesame. (Sherap tells me that the Calculus is a stone, or pebbly concretion, found in the brain or stomach of oxen and men; and that minium, which dictionaries give as red-lead, is a kind of paint of an orange colour.) The Drashidseje usually wear animal masks and are led in by Hashang, but on this occasion they were not present.

DU-DSEN, 2, demonic attendants on Ma-Ning: armed with bows, clad in red, monkey masks; perhaps the ghosts of discontented lamas.

DU-MO, 2, devils' wives, accompany Ma-Ning: long black hair and black gowns.

DURDAG, 4, graveyard ghouls: dressed in "tights" as skeletons with white bones on red ground; perhaps represent the scavengers who carried off King Langdarma's corpse after his assassination.

GARBA, 8, spirits from Zangdobelri, Pedma Sambhava's paradise in the south-west: wear the Jelwa Rignga and carry damaru and bells; aprons, necks, and wrists decorated with human skulls and bones.

GELONG, 2, attendants on Ma-Ning: in lama dress and flat gold hat.

GING, 8, spirits from Zangdobelri: carry drums.

GOMA, 4, janitor's attendant on Purba, with bird masks: carry purbu and skull.

GURUTSENJE, 8, the eight forms assumed by the Maha Guru Pedma Sambhava, of whom six are "mild," with human faces, and two "malignant": the latter occupy the seats at either end of the row, what we might call "corner-men," and represent the Guru in his aspect of fighting the Bön demons; they have pig masks and are accompanied by pigling sons.

HASHANG, the Master (Jintag), big head and big belly, a priest from China accompanied by two small boys; styled "The Dispenser of Gifts." He did not appear.

JEBA, 2, spirits of laymen, attendant on Ma-Ning: wear helmets with flags and carry swords.

JELJIN, one of the two kings of Lha: carries a biwang (a sort of banjo); probably the Hindu god Indra (Jupiter).

MA-NING, the chief Gönbo (Lord Demon) of the Nyimaba: snakes on his mask and rosary of human hearts.

PEDMA SAMBHAVA, the Guru Rinboche, from his paradise of Zangdobelri: wears gold fan; sits in middle of row of Gurutsen in "living statue" posture; right hand raised holding katam (p. 189), left hand holding skull-cup with tsebum inside it.

PURBA, Yidam (Demon King) of the Nyimaba, Dorje Shönu by name.

SAINTS, 14, in pig masks, attendant on Purba: purbu in right hand, skull-cup in left.

SHENBA, 2, the Merciless Killers, attendant on Ma-Ning: they are bare-legged, wear red night-caps and "shorts."

SOGJU, 10, bird masks attendant on Purba.

TROJU, 10, sweep demons out of courtyard with branches of bamboo.

TSANGBA, one of the two kings of Lha; has four faces; probably the Hindu god Brahma.

ZHANAG, 16, "Black Hats": carry purbu and skull.

ZHIDAG, evil spirits of the mountains: invisible.

In addition to the above are Purba's favourite attendants, The Crow and the Owl, the Deer and the Yak, and the Wolf, each of whom carries purbu and skull; and most important, The Stag, with sword and tö-trom (p. 190).

PARAPHERNALIA.

BUMBA—the baptismal kettle, usually of brass, with metal mirror attached, to spout, peacock feathers or kusha grass (i.e. grass from the sacred lake) as stopper; used to purify Pedma Sambhava.

DAMARU—small hand-drum made of two inverted skulls, like double egg-cup, usually covered with human skin; sometimes made of wood and covered with snake-skin; the skulls should be those of boy and girl (representing Bawo and Bamo) of not less than seven or more than ten years of age; has tasselled streamer and is sounded by twirling in hand, the tapping being done by little knobs of wood at the end of short strings, which are tied round its waist and flap over; used to attract the attention of gods, particularly when "giving power" at baptisms, etc.

DORMA—(1) made of dough, with black umbrella over it, surmounted by skull; entwined with intestines; during the seven days previous to the dance the lamas, invoking Purba, have invested it with evil spirits; (2) three dorma, representing a man, a woman, and a lama, who are to be sacrificed as a substitute for the people to the evil spirits of the country.

JELWA RIGNGA—the five Jinas or Celestial Buddhas (worn on the head in the form of a crown by Garba and Bamo).

KATAM—small trident decorated with three human heads; carried in the Guru's right hand.

LING-GA—mud or tsamba image of a man lying on his back with feet bound and arms above head, about 1½ feet long; invested by chief wizard with the hostile spirits of the past year; is cut up and eaten by The Stag, and the remains finally thrown to the four quarters.

MELONG—mirror of brass or silver attached to

Bumba; used to catch the reflection of Pedma Sambhava when being purified.

PURBU—wooden thunderbolt-dagger used for stabbing demons; is three edged, the handle being a dorje surmounted by three demon heads, with small horse's head on top representing Tamdin; used by Agba and Purba's followers.

TÖ-TROM—skull-stick, a dorje (thunder-bolt) surmounted by skull, a weapon carried by Stag.

TSEBUM—vase of life, made of brass or silver; holds the god of life, Tsebame (Aparmit), who is figured on the lid with horse's head in front of him, representing the tutelary demon Tamdin; round it is a rosary of tse-ril, pills of life; carried by Pedma Sambhava as emblematic of his having introduced tse-wang, life-power, into Tibet.

With these details explained the description of the show becomes much simplified.

We had been told that it would commence somewhere between eight and nine o'clock, but, making allowance for oriental customs, we arrived some time after nine. Nothing happened until some time after ten, when a number of lamas who had not been cast for parts filed out of the temple and offered chöba before the picture of Pedma Sambhava and purified him by baptism. By his kind visit to the world of men the Saint is held to have run the risk of contamination with evil; and such chances are obviated by a lama who catches his reflection in a metal mirror, melong, and pours a little saffron water on it. The drabas then proceed to the left-hand side of the courtyard, that is the Saint's left and our right, where they sit on the ground in rows, and during the next two days keep up a constant din, blowing trumpets and horns, large and small, beating drums and clashing cymbals almost without interval. Of the drums the most picturesque are those known as lag-nga, green drums perched on short poles and struck, by a sickle-shaped stick with a knob at the end. Some of the trumpets are over ten feet in length and require two men for their use.

The stage is now set and the performance begins.

ACT I.

Ten Troju masks come out of the temple and perform a slow dance, purging the courtyard of evil spirits by sweeping them out with branches of bamboos. When this has been done, the first of the celestial visitors, the Garba, of whom only six appear, dance in honour of the Saint and sing his praises. It is not a dance in the usual sense of the word but rather a posturing in slow time, and one could not hear any singing on account of the lamas' orchestra. The Garba are followed by the eight Ging who give a similar performance, and, when it is finished, the Garba return and petition Pedma Sambhava to appear.

ACT II.

Enter the Eight Gurutsen, and with them an extra form of the Guru, who occupies the middle position when they all sit down with their backs to the picture, ready to receive homage. The first act of homage is usually performed by Hashang, who comes in with his two boys and, as dispenser of gifts, leads in the masked figures, who represent the Eight Glorious Offerings. These of course stand, while Hashang is given a seat. The act was cut very short, as Hashang and the Drashidseje did not appear. The presentation of the Offerings was made in a modified form by kings Tsangba and Jeljin at the end of the next act; meanwhile the Gurutsen remained seated, waiting for further homage.

ACT III.

The five Bawo from Lha, who were down in the programme to open this act with a dance of homage to the saint, did not appear, but their consorts, the Bamo, came in and duly performed their turn. The cynosure of the crowd, however, is the cowherd and his wife, who come on in this act and are just as ridiculous as the clowns in a travelling circus at home. In a clumsy, bucolic way they keep offering milk to the Gurutsen and looking round for applause, and they remain on the stage throughout several acts, in fact until even this unsophisticated audience loses interest in them. At the end of the Bamo dance enter King Tsangba and his colleague King Jeljin from Lha, being the Indian gods Brahma and Indra, present Saint Pedma with a picture of the Eight Glorious Offerings, and thank him for the favour of his presence.

ACT IV.

In recognition of the homage thus paid, the Gurutsen now rise each in turn and dance a dignified measure, finally all treading the fantastic toe together. The central figure does not dance; he remains seated, gazing straight in front of him, his right hand raised holding the katam. His mask presents an extraordinarily beatific, not to say fatuous, expression, but he never moves hand or head the fraction of an inch during the performance, and doubtless feels proud as well as relieved when at last, with the eight others, he files back into the temple to a tremendously increased furore from the lamas' band. For the third and last time the Garba come in and dance, and, although one cannot hear it for the orchestra, sing a hymn of praise and thanks to Saint Pedma for his attendance.

ACT V.

Two Shenba come in and walk round the yard, blowing small trumpets and announcing the approach of the Gonbo Ma-Ning with his fiends and fiendesses.

ACT VI.

Enter Ma-Ning, Gönbo of the Nyima sect, with fourteen attendants in pairs, namely, Du-Dsen, Adsaras, Du-Mo, Gelong, Agba, Jeba, and Shenba. All are devils, and hold their jobs as Guardians of the Faith from Saint Pedma, in whose honour therefore they have come to dance. This is really the first devil-dance properly so-called; and as, when it was finished, time was getting on, a halt was called to the first day's proceedings.

When we all flocked into the courtyard next morning we found that the Guru's picture had been removed. In the middle of the yard was a tall mast hung with black flags of the Yidam, Chöjong, and Gönbo, some square, some triangular; but, as there was a strong wind blowing, all were made fast with ribbons of the usual five lucky colours, red, yellow, white, blue, and green. Like our May-pole, the mast may originally have had a phallic significance. In front of the mast was a table, on which was placed the dorma that the lamas had spent the previous week in investing with evil spirits. Under the table were three more dorma, representing a man, a woman, and a lama. Beyond the mast lay the Ling-ga. In the courtyard a special tent had been pitched for the Agba, who was chief wizard, to save his fine clothes from the dust, for he was too busy always to be going into the temple, and the clothes used in the dance are of great value and are preserved in the lamasery for years against this annual festival.

The second is the Agba's busy day, and, while we wait for the actors to get ready, he comes out of his tent and performs a dignified dance.

ACT VII.

This act is a preparation for the advent of Purba, the chief tutelary of the Nyima sect, a much more powerful personage even than Ma-Ning, who is one of his Lord Demons.

First enter four skeleton forms, Durdag, whose white bones stand out on a red ground. They are graveyard ghouls, have large ears, and in dancing round find devils in all sorts of unexpected places and are energetic in their pursuit.

Next enter sixteen Agba, wizards or sorcerers, cunning at detecting demons where the ordinary man sees nothing, popularly known as "Black Hats" (Zhanag) from the colour of their broad head-gear. As they perform their dance, two lamas come from the temple, one with a tray of silver bowls, from which he hands a bowl to each Black Hat. The other carries a silver tea-pot, from which he fills the bowls with tea or with beer. While the lamas at the side of the courtyard, with renewed vigour, beat their drums and blow their trumpets, the Black Hats hold the bowls on high and call upon the Zhidag to accept the offering (serchem). As the latter remain invisible, the Black Hats throw the serchem into the air, returning the bowls to the lamas. They then conclude their dance and retire.

Then come in, led by a small boy, two of Purba's pets, masked as a Deer and a Yak, who perform a dance.

Next come four bird masks, Purba's doorkeepers (Goma), who also dance; and finally his special janitors, the Crow and the Owl, who dance.

The eight last-mentioned creatures, as well as the Black Hats, all carry the devil-stabbing purbu. Finally enters the chief wizard who, with forefinger and thumb in his mouth, calls up the devils by whistling.

ACT VIII.

Enter Purba (Dorje Shönu), accompanied by his six doorkeepers, fourteen saints (mostly in pig masks), the yak, the deer, and his pet wolf, twenty-three attendants in all, each with a purbu. Purba thanks Saint Pedma for his presence and begs for continued help in the coming year. All join in dance.

A man brings in a low table, which he places behind the mast and on it lays the Ling-ga, with a skin rug in front of it. The chief wizard whistles the disobedient and hostile spirits into the Ling-ga.

ACT IX.

The Stag comes in with tö-trom in his hand. He slowly approaches the Ling-ga and, laying down the tö-trom on the skin, picks up a sword. He sharpens the sword in the air and dances round, a long, slow dance. Eventually he returns and, sitting on the skin, cuts up the Ling-ga with great zest and eats its flesh and drinks its blood with gusto, finally throwing pieces to the four points of the compass. There can be little doubt that this is a relic of the human sacrifices, attended with cannibalism, which were made to the Bön devils whom Saint Pedma drove out or won over. Each year brings forth evil spirits; the more docile are incorporated with the guardians of the faith, the obstinate and rebellious are either cut up with the ling-ga or burned with the dorma. The Stag ends his performance with contortions on the skin rug in an ecstasy of blood-drunkenness.

ACT X.

Re-enter Purba and his twenty-three attendants, who join in a dance and, while dancing, receive from the lamas remnants of the ling-ga, which they hold for a while and then cast to the four quarters, signifying that the evil spirits that sought to work harm to the Guru's religion have been thrown to the demons.

This is the last act within the lamasery, and presents are now brought in and exhibited at the foot of the mast. On this occasion they formed a very small heap, owing to the absence of the local officials. However, twenty packages of brick-tea arrived from the British Consulate and fifteen from the magistrate, each of which yamens sent ninety-four kadas or ceremonial scarves. From the number of kadas sent one can estimate more or less accurately the number of lama participants in the show.

ACT XI.

The sixteen Black Hats lead a mob of lamas and onlookers in carrying off all the dorma, both the one in which evil spirits have been invested and the three which are substitutes for the lamas and laity, to a straw hut near the river. While the lamas read incantations and blow their trumpets, the chief wizard slings three stones and shoots three arrows into the hut, which is then set on fire. So to the wizard's whistling and the lamas' drum-beating the dorma go up in smoke to the evil spirits of the country. Like the cutting-up of the ling-ga, the burning of the dorma seems to be a relic of the human sacrifices of pre-Buddhist days.

* * * * * *

NOTE.—The above is a description of the dance as presented by the Red or Unreformed sect, whose creed is descended in the direct line from Saint Pedma Sambhava, the founder of Lamaism in the eighth century. It is not always exactly as described; conventional variations recur periodically. The Geluba or Yellow sect, the established church of Tibet, has a very similar dance on the 28th of the 6th moon (29th July, 1924), the feast-day of Jelje Dorje Shugden and Baldan Lhamo. Shugden was a very learned lama who, having displeased the Tibetan Government, was condemned to be thrown into the river; his angry spirit had in due course to be placated by being made a Jelbo, and he is now worshipped by the Geluba and the Sachyaba as one of the greatest of their Chöjong. Baldan Lhamo, the terrible Magzorma, is the goddess who was supposed to be reincarnated in the late Queen Victoria. The dance, which also lasts two days, and differs from the other chiefly in the fact that all the actors represent real devils, was held at a lamasery in the Mi-nyag country over the Jedo, several days' journey "outside the barrier," and, while unable to attend it personally, I succeeded in obtaining the following particulars from the Geluba lamas who staged it.

In the courtyard on the first day was displayed a portrait of Tsongkaba, the lama who, after hearing the gospel of "the man with the big nose," apparently a missionary from the Occident, about A.D. 1400, reorganised the Kadamba and brought about the predominance of the Yellow sect. It is not invariably Tsongkaba who is thus honoured by the Geluba; sometimes it is Jamba (Maitreya), the Coming Buddha. The Geluba take small account of Saint Pedma.

As in the other dance, the initial ceremony consists in cleansing the courtyard of evil spirits by four Adsaras, who wear the masks and dress of Hindus.

Following this, enter a number of Shugden's attendants. Two Du-mo (fiendesses with black faces and dress and long black hair), armed with swords, come in from an apparently successful raid on demons, whose lungs and hands they bring as an offering to Shugden; and two Black Hats, with purbu and skull-cup, offer tea to Shugden. Other attendants are two Tiger masks with swords and lances, two Goma, the Owl and the Crow, two Garudas or Phœnixes, who are numbered among the minor deities, with swords and skulls, two Jelbo, angry spirits that had been deified, and two Dsimara carrying umbrellas and lances. Shugden then appears holding human lungs and heart, with four servants equipped with swords and hammers. All dance together, Shugden joining in, and Shugden's gangso or sacred book is read by lamas to the accompaniment of drums, cymbals, and trumpets.

The attendants then file out in pairs, leaving Shugden and his four servants to welcome Baldan Lhamo, who enters with tö-trom and skull-cup full of blood, accompanied by five Lhamo. She is an unprepossessing, formidable creature, the only sign of the weakness of her sex being that she sports a peacock feather. Twelve more Lhamo arrive from "the snow mountains," and perhaps the sex is again betrayed by all accepting tea from the lamas. All then retire, except Baldan Lhamo and her five attendants.

The first day ends with a dance of seven Gönbo.

On the second day the courtyard is furnished with a Chöjong-mast, Dorma, and Ling-ga in the way already described. During the seven days of preparation the lamas had invoked the assistance of Damjen Chöjel in investing the Dorma with evil spirits.

Enter the great Chöjong of the Geluba, Damjen Chöjel with his consort, four servants, and eight Adsaras. After they have danced, a lama recites from Damjen's gangso.

Damjen then proceeds to put the evil spirits into the ling-ga, as the chief wizard had done at Dorje Drag, and, while he whistles, a lama helps to attract them by waving a black flag. When this ceremony is completed to their satisfaction they all leave, and the Stag comes in and cuts up the ling-ga.

Sixteen Black Hats with purbus and skulls enter and dance; the lamas bring them tea, which they offer to the Zhidag, and give each Black Hat a piece of the ling-ga.

On the departure of the Black Hats, the lamas perform a dance with cymbals and drums. After the dance, the Black Hats again join them and the crowd helps to drag out the dorma and commit them to the flames.

APPENDIX I

TABLE OF TUTELARY DEMONS MENTIONED IN THE TEXT.

	YIDAM (Demon Kings and Queens)	CHÖJONG (Demon Generals)	GÖNBO (Lord Demons)
GELUBA	Dorje Jigje (Vajra Bhairava)	Damjen Tamdin (Hayagriva) Dsimara	
KARJUBA	Dorje Pamo (Vajra Varahi)	Damjen	
SACHYABA	Dorje Shönu (Purba)	Baldan Lhamo (Magzorma) Shugden	
NYIMABA	Dorje Shönu (Purba)	Za (Zachabjug) Damjen Lhamo Genema (Ekadsati)	Ma-Ning

APPENDIX II

Stages on Roads across Tibet from Tachienlu to Lhasa.

I—North Road ("Merchants'" Road).

Tachienlu — Jedo — Tramtrun — Bayu Dronggo —Bame — Shaboshi — Jesodrong — Miju Nagnang —Koja — DAWU — Zhartang — Juselato — Sharatang — Drago — Jale — Drebo Karsar — Katsalada (Dsigugun) — KANZE (Kartsi) — Beru — RONGBATSA — Chudsitang — YILHUNG Lharigar — Lhaja — Chematang (Norbu Dratrug) — Lingtsong (Guze) — Namjelgun — Tritogun — Drölma Lhakang — Chöden Podrang — Sidrongba — Druchu Druka — Seo — Damtogun — Karsar Janggun — Baltang Lianroba — Benchengunba — JYEKUNDO (Jekudo) — Baltang Tanggo — Porolatsa — Dsombu Chudri — Churuka — Gesar Dapen — Sashozhung — Baldon — Lanyi — Dsachuka — Shodrulatsa — Zaberkardo — Nachenma — Gungmori — Damzhung — Yangdozhung — Sanalatsa — Dsatrakar — Kalmanyishar — Shachuka — Chang Kunang — Gamezhung — Chöba Dingan — NAGCHUKA — Samye Gozhu — Jichaka — Tsaka — Bumatang — Lanyi — Jarongnang — Zhudu — Sharada — Galden Chökor — Bomdo — Lhasa.

II—Pilgrims' Road.

Kanze — Rongbatsa — Yilhung — DSOGCHEN — Lingtsong — DENKO — Druchu Druka — Druko — LHOKO — Lhotrido — NANGCHEN — Rongbo Dseratang — RIWOCHE — Chado — Gojo — Draya — Chungbo Garru—Chungbonagru—NAGSHE—Chungbo

Sertsako — GONGBO — DAGBO — Zharsang Angchöling — Dagbo Ehzhung — Yardo Drala — Yarlung — TSETANG — SAMYE — Gungala — Lhasa.

III—SOUTH ROAD ("Chinese Amban's" Road).

Tachienlu — Jedo — Dizu — Anyag — Golotang — Oroshi — Nyachuka (HOKOW) — Magendrong — Shigolo — Trama Radong — Horchuka — LITANG — Dotang — Dzogarmo — Lamaya — Neda — Drati — Dashe — Bangtramo — Bajoshi — BATANG — Drobalung — Dagateng — Kongdziteng — Bome — Bomdo — MARKAM — Rito — Aratang — Dotramka —Odze — Goatang — Lojadzung — Alado — DRAYA —Yosa — Langdi — Zhugo —Wakar — Sangdodzo — Bagong — Bambeng — Mongzhu — Shongida — CHAMDO — Guroshi — Lada — Lagong — Nganda — Bako — Mari — Zhayezam — Hodzong — Dzito — Shodo — Bare — Lhadse — Balbar — Ujandada — Namjelgun — Ngandroge — Alado — Jagong — Aladotu — Dsachuka — Harigo — Ardza — Golewa — Drado — Larugo — JAMDA — Gam — Numari — Tsongmora — Ozejang — Rinling — Medrongegar — Dechen — Lhasa.

(Chinese estimate the length of this route as 5,210 *li*, roughly 1,740 English miles.)

INDEX